**기초영어 1000문장 말하기 연습 4**

박미진 지음

이제 지겨운 '공부'는 그만하고,
'연습'으로 말문을 틔우자!

# 기초영어 1000문장 말하기연습

토마토
출판사

# 이 책의 활용

**Speaking Practice** - 한국어를 영어로 전환하는 영작 연습

1. 한 페이지에 10문항씩 있어요. 한 문항을 보고 이해하는데 3초, 생각하고 말하는데 3초, 그렇게 한 문항당 6초를 소비한다면, 한 페이지에 1분, 100문항을 10분 안에 만드는 연습을 할 수 있어요.
2. 강의를 들으면서 함께해요. 집중하는데 도움도 되고 이해하기도 더 쉬울 거예요.
3. 이제 혼자 말하면서 연습을 해보아요! 녹음기를 켜고 하면 나의 발음도 체크하고, 시간도 체크할 수 있으니 일석이조겠죠?
4. 이제 책의 맨 뒷장을 펴고 정답을 확인해 보아요. 강의 들으며 입으로 모양을 만들어 보면서 한 번, 글로 보고 다시 말하면서 두 번, 답 맞추면서 세 번, 이렇게 한 문항을 세 번이나 반복할 수 있어요!
5. 시간이 있다면 마지막엔 글로도 써보세요! 만약 쓰기가 힘들다면 강의를 다시 들으면서 꾸준히 반복적으로 훈련해 보는 것도 좋겠네요!

## Review – 지금까지 배운 요소를 구분하는 연습

1. 여기는 처음부터 빠르게 변환하려고 하지 말고, 문장 속의 요소를 구분하는 연습이 필요해요. 한 문장씩 차근차근 읽어보고, 영어로 어떻게 말하는지 생각해 보고, 천천히 말하는 연습을 해요.
2. 쓰면서 다시 생각해 보는 연습을 해요.
3. 답을 확인해 보아요.

## Dialogue Practice – 실제 상황에서의 응용

1. 영어를 먼저 읽어보아요!
2. 문장을 보면서 이게 배운 것 중에서 어떤 부분에 해당되는지 생각해 봐요! (want to 인지, have to 인지 등등) 이렇게 구분만 할 수 있어도 너무 좋아요!
3. 영어가 익숙해지면, 뒤 페이지에 있는 한국어를 보며 입으로 영작에 도전해 보아요!

## [힌트]와 괄호의 활용

힌트가 있는 문항이 있어요. 힌트를 보고 문장을 만들어요. 영어 문장을 떠올리는데도 도움되고, 적을 때는 스펠링도 도움이 되어서, 단어를 직접 찾아보는데 시간을 소요할 필요가 없어요!

한국말을 자연스럽게 표현하면서, 생략된 단어나 직역한 표현들을 괄호 안에 넣어두었어요. 괄호의 내용을 활용해서 문장을 만들어 보세요!

# 목차

| Unit 0 | 시작하기 | 010 |
| Unit 1 | 상대의 말에 동의하고 싶을 때 "나도" So do I. Neither can I. | 018 |
| Unit 2 | 상대의 말에 리액션 하고 싶을 때 "그래? 정말?" Do you? Are you? | 040 |
| Unit 3 | 주인공을 물어보는 질문을 하고 싶을 때 "누가? 뭐가?" Subject Questions | 062 |
| Unit 4 | 확인을 위해서 부정의 질문을 하고 싶을 때 "안 해?" Negative Questions | 084 |
| Unit 5 | 과거 이전의 일을 말하고 싶을 때 "했었어" had p.p. | 106 |
| Unit 6 | 상대에게 바라는 걸 말하고 싶을 때 "하면 좋겠어" I want you to | 128 |
| Unit 7 | 누군가 (하라고) 한 말을 전달하고 싶을 때 "하라고 했어" 간접화법 1 | 150 |
| Unit 8 | 누군가 했던 말을 전달하고 싶을 때 "했다고 했어" 간접화법 2 | 172 |
| Unit 9 | 누군가 물어봤던 말을 전달하고 싶을 때 "했냐고 물어봤어" 간접화법 3 | 194 |
| Unit 10 | 알고 보니 아닌 현재 사실의 반전을 말하고 싶을 때 "한 줄 알았어" I thought | 216 |

정답체크     238

# Unit

# 0

시작하기

# Unit 0
## 시작하기

### 기초영어 1000문장 말하기 연습 1권

| Positive (긍정) | Negative (부정) | Question (의문) |
|---|---|---|
| I want to<br>I'd like to | I don't want to<br>I wouldn't like to | Do you want to?<br>Would you like to? |
| 할래, 하고 싶어 | 안 할래, 하기 싫어 | 할래? 하고 싶어? |
| I have to | I don't have to | Do I have to? |
| 해야 돼, 해야 해 (의무) | 안 해도 돼 | 해야 돼? |
| I can | I can't | Can you? |
| 할 수 있어 | 못해, 할 수 없어 | 할 수 있어? 해줄래? (부탁) |
| You can | You can't | Can I? |
| 해도 돼 (허락) | 하면 안 돼 | 해도 돼? |
| I will | I won't | Shall I? |
| 할게 | 안 할게 | 할까? (제안) |
| I should | I shouldn't | Should I? |
| 해야지, 하는 게 좋겠다 | 안 하는 게 좋겠다 | 하는 게 좋을까? |
| I think I should | I don't think I should | Do you think I should? |
| 하는 게 좋을 것 같아 | 안 하는 게 좋을 것 같아 | 하는 게 좋을 것 같아? |
| I'm going to | I'm not going to | Are you going to? |
| 할 거야 | 안 할 거야 | 할 거야? |

# 기초영어 1000문장 말하기 연습 2권

| Positive (긍정) | Negative (부정) | Question (의문) |
|---|---|---|
| I'm -ing | I'm not -ing | Are you-ing? |
| 해, 하고 있어 (지금) | 안 해, 하는 거 아니야 | 해? 하고 있어? |
| I 동사 | I don't | Do you? |
| 해 (원래) | 안 해 | 해? |
| He will | He won't | Will he? |
| 할걸, 할 거야 (예측) | 안 할걸, 안 할 거야 | 할까? |
| I think I'll | I don't think I'll | Do you think I'll? |
| 할 것 같아 | 안 할 것 같아 | 할 것 같아? |
| I may/might | I may not/might not | May I? |
| 할지도 몰라, 할 수도 있어 | 안 할지도 몰라 | 해도 돼요? (허락) |
| I 과거 | I didn't | Did you? |
| 했어, 했었어 | 안 했어, 안 했었어 | 했어? 했었어? |
| I was -ing | I wasn't -ing | Were you -ing? |
| 하고 있었어 (그때) | 안 하고 있었어 | 하고 있었어? |
| I have p.p. | I haven't p.p. | Have you p.p.? |
| 했어, 해봤어<br>해왔어 (쭉) | 안 했어, 안 해봤어<br>안 한 지~됐어 | 했어? 해봤어?<br>한 지~됐어? |
| I could | I couldn't | Could you? Could I? |
| 할 수 있었어 | 못 했어, 할 수 없었어 | 해줄래? 해도 돼? |
| I would | I wouldn't | Would you? |
| (나라면) 할 거야 | (나라면) 안 할 거야 | (너라면) 할 거야? |

# 기초영어 1000문장 말하기 연습 3권

| Positive (긍정) | Negative (부정) | Question (의문) |
|---|---|---|
| 동사 | Don't | - |
| 해, 하세요 | 하지 마, 하지 마세요 | - |
| I used to | I didn't use to | Did you use to? |
| 예전엔 했었는데 (지금은 안 해) | 예전엔 안 했었는데 (지금은 해) | 예전에 했었어? |
| I was going to | I wasn't going to | Were you going to? |
| 하려고 했었는데 (안 했어) | 안 하려고 했었는데 (했어) | 하려고 했었어? |
| There is/are | There isn't/aren't | Is/Are there? |
| 있어 | 없어 | 있어? |
| There was/were | There wasn't/weren't | Was/Were there? |
| 있었어 | 없었어 | 있었어? |
| There will be | There won't be | Will there be? |
| 있을 거야 | 없을 거야 | 있을까? |
| I know what I need. | I don't know what I need. | Do you know what I need? |
| 내가 뭐 필요한지 알아 | 내가 뭐 필요한지 몰라 | 내가 뭐 필요한지 알아? |
| Tell me if I have to~ | I don't know if I have to~ | Can you tell me if I have to~? |
| 내가 해야 되는지 말해줘 (혹시) | 내가 해야 되는 건지 몰라 | 내가 해야 되는지 말해줄래? |

| 긍정문, 부정 tag | 부정문, 긍정 tag | - |
|---|---|---|
| 하지? (그렇지?) | 안 하지? | - |
| I have been -ing | I haven't been -ing | Have you been -ing? |
| 하고 있었어 (지금)<br>했어 (계속) | 안 하고 있었어<br>안 한 지~됐어 | 하고 있었어?<br>한 지~됐어? |

| It is | It isn't | Is it? | 지금, 원래 |
|---|---|---|---|
| It was | It wasn't | Was it? | 그때, 전에 |
| It will be | It won't be | Will it be? | 예측 |
| It's going to be | It isn't going to be | Is it going to be? | 계획 |
| It might be | It might not be | - | 추측, 가능성 |
| It has to be | It doesn't have to be | Does it have to be? | 의무 |
| It has been | It hasn't been | Has it been? | 지금, 쭉, 계속 |
| It would be | It wouldn't be | Would it be? | (만일)그러면 (~하겠다) |
| It used to be | It didn't use to be | Did it use to be? | 예전에는, 옛날에는 |
| It was going to be | It wasn't going to be | Was it going to be? | 그럴 뻔/그럴 거였는데 |

# Unit

# 1

상대의 말에
동의하고 싶을 때

# Unit 1
## 상대의 말에 동의하고 싶을 때

## So do I. Neither do I. "나도"

상대가 한 말에 동의할 때 자주 사용되는 "나도" 라는 표현은 "so" 나 "neither" 를 사용해서 짧고, 간단하게 만들 수 있어요. 문장은 보통 주어와 동사 순으로 이루어지는데, 문장 자체를 생략하고, 상대가 말한 동일한 시제나 조동사를 사용하면서 주어 동사의 순서가 바뀌는 도치가 일어납니다!

| Positive (긍정) | Negative (부정) |
|---|---|
| So do I.<br>So am I.<br>Etc. | Neither do I.<br>Neither am I.<br>Etc. |
| 나도 ||

긍정문에 대한 동의를 할 때는 "So" 를 사용하고, 부정문에 대한 동의는 "Neither" 를 사용해요. 또한, 상대의 한 말에 대한 동의이므로, 상대가 사용한 시제나, 조동사를 동일하게 사용해 주면 됩니다.
"So" 나 "Neither" 를 사용해서 "나도" 뿐만 아니라 "너도" 역시도 만들 수 있어요. "So do you." "Neither can you." 이렇게요!

**이렇게 만듭니다!**

So/Neither + 조동사 + I

조동사는 상대가 사용한 문장에서 쓰였던 적절한 동사를 넣어주면 돼요!

|  | Positive (긍정) | Negative (부정) |
|---|---|---|
| be 동사 | I am hungry.<br>-So am I. | I'm not hungry.<br>-Neither am I. |
|  | I was tired.<br>-So was I. | I wasn't tired.<br>-Neither was I. |
| 조동사 | I can do it.<br>-So can I. | I can't do it.<br>-Neither can I. |
|  | I will do it.<br>-So will I. | I won't do it.<br>-Neither will I. |
| 현재 | I like this.<br>-So do I. | I don't like this.<br>-Neither do I. |
| 과거 | I liked it.<br>-So did I. | I didn't like it.<br>-Neither did I. |
| 현재완료 | I have been there.<br>-So have I. | I haven't been there.<br>-Neither have I. |

<주의>

Neither 대신에 Nor 도 사용할 수 있어요!

하지만, Neither 나 Nor 둘 다 부정 단어라서, 뒤에는 **긍정** 조동사를 사용합니다.

<"나도"를 나타내는 다른 표현들>

| 긍정 | 부정 |
|---|---|
| Me, too. | Me, neither. |
| I'm hungry, too.<br>I like it, too. | I'm not hungry, either.<br>I don't like it, either. |
| I do, too. / I am, too.<br>I did, too. / Etc. | I don't, either. / I'm not, either.<br>I didn't, either. / Etc. |

# Speaking Practice
## 1min

### 긍정문
☞ 오른쪽 힌트를 이용해서, 직접 문장을 만들어보세요!

훈련용 강의 바로 듣기

정답확인 : P 238

| 01 | (나) 밖에 나가서 뭔가 하고 싶어.<br>-나도. 우리 뭐 할까? | |
| --- | --- | --- |
| 02 | 너무 피곤해.<br>-나도. 우리 그만 마치는 게 좋겠다. | [마치다, 그만하다<br>call it a night] |
| 03 | 나 이거 좋아해.<br>-나도. 우리 비슷한 점이 많아. (공통점이 많아) | [비슷한 점/공통점이 많다<br>have so much in common] |
| 04 | 나 일찍 나가야 돼.<br>-우리도. 넌 몇 시에 나갈 거야? | |
| 05 | 널 봐서 너무 행복했어.<br>-나도. | |
| 06 | 나 그거 정말 즐거웠어. 좋은 시간 보냈어.<br>-나도. 너무 좋았어. | [정말 so much] |
| 07 | 나 거기 많이 (여러 번) 가봤어.<br>-나도. 내가 가장 좋아하는 곳이야. | [많이, 여러 번 many times<br>가장 좋아하는 곳<br>one's favorite spot] |
| 08 | 알아.<br>-나도. | |
| 09 | 우리 늦었었어.<br>-나도. 모두 늦었었어. | |
| 10 | 나 그거 고칠 수 있어.<br>-나도. 네가 할래, 아니면 내가 하는 게 좋을까? | |

# Speaking Practice  1min

## 긍정문

☞ 오른쪽 힌트를 이용해서, 직접 문장을 만들어보세요!

| | | |
|---|---|---|
| 11 | 난 우리 새 프로젝트(에 대해) 정말 기대돼.<br>-나도. 잘 될 것 같아. | [기대되는 excited<br>잘 될것 같은, 조짐 좋은, 희망적인 promising] |
| 12 | 나 어렸을 때 이거 정말 좋아했었는데.<br>-나도. | |
| 13 | 나 이 영화 보고 싶어.<br>-나도. 이걸로 보자, 그럴까? | |
| 14 | 나 이거 고르려고 했었는데.<br>-나도. 모두가 이걸 원했어. | |
| 15 | 나 그거 벌써 봤어.<br>-나도. | |
| 16 | 언젠가 남미에 가고 싶어.<br>-나도. 남미 어느 부분 여행하고 싶어? | [언젠가 one day<br>~부분 part of ] |
| 17 | 난 될 때까지 기다릴 수 있어.<br>-나도야. 덤벼봐. | [시간이 얼마나 걸리든, 될 때까지 as long as it takes<br>해보자, 덤벼봐 Bring it on!] |
| 18 | 어젯밤에 영화 보러 갔었어.<br>-나도. 넌 무슨 영화 봤어? | [영화 보러 가다<br>go to the movies] |
| 19 | 내가 그 애라면 그거 할 텐데.<br>-나도. 난 그 애가 그냥 이해가 안 돼. | |
| 20 | 전 그분을 만나고 싶어요.<br>-저도요. | |

Unit 1

# Speaking Practice 1min

## 긍정문

☞ 오른쪽 힌트를 이용해서, 직접 문장을 만들어보세요!

| 21 | 미안해. 내가 틀렸었어.<br>-나도. 사과하지 않아도 돼. | |
| --- | --- | --- |
| 22 | 고맙다고 말하고 싶었어.<br>-나도. 그리고 그렇게 말해줘서 고마워. | |
| 23 | 나 그를 도와주려고 했었는데.<br>-우리도. 그건 너무 늦었었어. | |
| 24 | 그 애한테 전화한다는 게.<br>-나도. 그냥 시간이 없었어. | [~할 마음/의향/생각이다 mean to] |
| 25 | 배고팠어.<br>-나도. | |
| 26 | 나 그거(에 대해) 완전히 까먹고 있었어.<br>-나도. | [완전히 totally] |
| 27 | 나 시간 좀 남아.<br>-나도. | [시간 남다, 여유 있다 have time to kill] |
| 28 | 나 그 애 안 지 오래됐어.<br>-나도. 한 10년 됐어. | |
| 29 | 생각해 볼게.<br>-나도. 나중에 결정하자(하룻밤 생각해 보자), 그럴까? | [나중에 결정하다, 하룻밤 생각해 보다 sleep on it] |
| 30 | 난 그 애가 정말 그리워.<br>-나도. 그리고 모두도. | |

## 긍정문

☞ 오른쪽 힌트를 이용해서, 직접 문장을 만들어보세요!

| | | |
|---|---|---|
| 31 | 너 오늘 멋져 보여.<br>-너도! | |
| 32 | 너 정말 아름다워.<br>-너도. | |
| 33 | 너 정말 잘했어.<br>-너도. 좋은 게임이었어. | [잘하다<br>do a good/great job] |
| 34 | 너 멋졌어!<br>-너도. 난 네가 정말 자랑스러워. | [멋진, 대단한 amazing] |
| 35 | 난 다시 일하러 가야겠다. 그리고 너도. | [다시 일하러 가다, 하던 일하다<br>get back to work] |
| 36 | 너 피곤해 보여.<br>-너도. | |
| 37 | 너 나한테 거짓말했잖아.<br>-너도 그랬잖아. | [거짓말하다 lie to] |
| 38 | 너 (정말) 열심히 했잖아.<br>-모두 다 그래. | [열심히 하다 work hard] |
| 39 | 그 애가 관심 있어 할 거 같아.<br>-나도. | |
| 40 | 그 애도 이거 해보면 좋아할 거야.<br>그리고 너도. | |

Unit 1

## Speaking Practice 1min

### 긍정문

☞ 오른쪽 힌트를 이용해서, 직접 문장을 만들어보세요!

| 41 | 나 이거 쉽게 할 수 있어. 그리고 너도. | |
| --- | --- | --- |
| 42 | 그가 널 도와줄걸. 그리고 나도 그럴 거고. | |
| 43 | 그래, 나 그거 했어. 그리고 너도 했잖아. | |
| 44 | 그 애 그거 있어. 그리고 나도. 너 언제든 빌려도 돼. | [언제든 any time] |
| 45 | 너의 아빠가 네 걱정 많이 해. 그리고 나도 그렇고. | |
| 46 | 그 애 울고 있었어. 그리고 나도. 그거 가슴 아팠어. | [가슴 아픈 heartbreaking] |
| 47 | 그 앤 네가 멋지다고 생각해. 그리고 나도. 그거 잊지 마. | |
| 48 | 나 거기 있었어. 그리고 그 애도. | |
| 49 | Mary는 이거 좋아해. 그리고 그녀의 남편도. | |
| 50 | 그 애 요리 잘해, 그리고 피터도. | [요리 잘하는 a good/great cook] |

## Speaking Practice 1min

### 부정문

☞ 오른쪽 힌트를 이용해서, 직접 문장을 만들어보세요!

| | | |
|---|---|---|
| 51 | 난 모르는 일이야. (난 그거에 대해 아무것도 몰라) <br> -나도 마찬가지야. | |
| 52 | 나 화난 거 아니야. <br> -나도. | |
| 53 | 기억이 안 나. (기억 못 해) <br> -나도. | |
| 54 | 난 거기 안 갈 거야. <br> -나도야. | |
| 55 | 난 아무 말도 안 했어. <br> -나도. | |
| 56 | 나 아무한테도 말한 적 없어. <br> -나도. | |
| 57 | 나 아무 말도 못 했어. <br> -나도 그랬어. | |
| 58 | 거기 안 가본 지 정말 오래됐다. <br> -나도. | [정말 오래 for ages] |
| 59 | 나 농담하는 거 아니야. <br> -나도야. 진짜야. (난 진짜 심각해) | [진짜인, 진심인, 심각한 dead serious] |
| 60 | 난 이거 별로야. (난 이거 좋아하지 않아) <br> -나도야. | |

## Speaking Practice  1min

### 부정문

☞ 오른쪽 힌트를 이용해서, 직접 문장을 만들어보세요!

| | | |
|---|---|---|
| 61 | 가고 싶지 않아.<br>-나도, 하지만 우리 그래야 돼. | |
| 62 | 난 그러고 싶지 않았어.<br>-나도 그랬어. | |
| 63 | 거기 안 가봤어.<br>-나도. | |
| 64 | 전혀 피곤하지 않았어.<br>-나도. | [전혀 at all] |
| 65 | 이거 혼자 못하겠어.<br>-나도. 우리 이거 같이 하는 게 좋겠다. | |
| 66 | 그 애 안 올 것 같아.<br>-나도 그래. | |
| 67 | 아무한테도 말 안 할게.<br>-나도. 약속해. | |
| 68 | 나 그거 다 못했어.<br>-나도. 시간이 부족했어. (충분한 시간이 없었어) | [다하다 finish] |
| 69 | 나라면 안 해.<br>-나도. 그게 모든 걸 망칠지도 몰라. | [망치다 ruin] |
| 70 | 내가 안 했어.<br>-나도. | |

# Speaking Practice 1min

## 부정문

☞ 오른쪽 힌트를 이용해서, 직접 문장을 만들어보세요!

| 71 | 그렇게 오래는 못 기다려.<br>-나도 그래. | [그렇게 오래 that long] |
|---|---|---|
| 72 | 그건 생각 못 했네. (그거에 대해 생각해 보지 않았어)<br>-나도. | |
| 73 | 나 이거 안 썼는데.<br>-나도. | |
| 74 | 나 내일 일 안 해도 돼.<br>-나도. 뭐라도 같이 할래? | |
| 75 | 나 마음 안 바꿀 거야.<br>-나도. | |
| 76 | 정말 끔찍했어. 싫었어. (난 그게 좋지 않았어)<br>-나도. | |
| 77 | 나 지금 별거 안 하는데.<br>-나도. 커피 한잔할래? | [별거, 별로 much]<br>커피 한잔하다 grab a coffee] |
| 78 | 그거 안 될 거 같아.<br>-나도. 우리 어떡하지? (뭘 하는 게 좋을까?) | |
| 79 | 난 준비되지 않았었어.<br>-나도 솔직히, 준비된 사람 없었어. (아무도 준비되지 않았었어) | [솔직히 frankly] |
| 80 | 몰랐어.<br>-나도. 마음이 너무 안 좋다. | [마음 안 좋다 feel (so) bad] |

Unit 1

# Speaking Practice
## 1min

### 부정문
☞ 오른쪽 힌트를 이용해서, 직접 문장을 만들어보세요!

| | | |
|---|---|---|
| 81 | 나 이럴(이걸 위한) 시간 없어.<br>-나도 마찬가지야. 우리 더 이상의 시간을 낭비하지 않는 게 좋겠어. | [더 이상의 시간<br>any more time] |
| 82 | 난 지금까지 아무 문제 없었어.<br>-나도 그랬어. | [아무 문제<br>any problems] |
| 83 | 난 결혼할 준비가 안 되어 있어.<br>-나도야. | [결혼하다 get married] |
| 84 | 나 예전엔 이거 안 좋아했었는데.<br>-나도. 그게 정들었어. | [점점 좋아지다, 정들다<br>grow on sb] |
| 85 | 내 생각은 달라. (난 그렇게 보지 않아)<br>-나도. 우리 생각이 같네. | [그렇게 that way<br>생각이 같은<br>on the same page] |
| 86 | 어젯밤에 잠 전혀 못 잤어.<br>-나도. | [전혀 at all] |
| 87 | 나 기다리는 거 괜찮아.<br>-우리도. | [괜찮다, 상관없다<br>don't mind -ing] |
| 88 | 너 자신을 자책하지 않는 게 좋겠어.<br>-알아. 너도 마찬가지야. | [자책하다 blame oneself] |
| 89 | 난 그들에 대해 충분히 잘 알지 못해.<br>-나도. | [충분히 잘 well enough] |
| 90 | 난 저애가 무슨 말을 하고 있는 건지 이해를 못 하겠어.<br>-나도. 말도 안 되는 소리하고 있어. | [말도 안 되는 소리하다<br>talk nonsense] |

## Speaking Practice  1min

### 부정문
☞ 오른쪽 힌트를 이용해서, 직접 문장을 만들어보세요!

| | | |
|---|---|---|
| 91 | 그 애 이거 필요 없고, 너도 마찬가지야. | |
| 92 | 너 여기 있으면 안 돼(여기 있지 않는 게 좋겠어), 그리고 쟤도. | |
| 93 | 그 애는 아무 말도 안 할 거고, 나도 그럴 거야. | |
| 94 | 그 애는 이거 안 먹어, 그리고 Jim도. | |
| 95 | 그들은 아무것도 가져오지 않아도 되고, 너도야. | |
| 96 | Nick은 여기 없어. 그리고 Sue도. | |
| 97 | 나도 그거에 대해 기분 별로였고, Kelly도 그랬어. | [기분 좋은, 만족스러운 happy about ] |
| 98 | 그 애도 아무것도 하기 싫어하고, 나도 그래. | |
| 99 | 저 전화기도 안 되고, 이것도 그러네. | |
| 100 | 난 오늘 이후로 이거에 대해 다시는 절대 이야기 안 할게. 그리고 너도. 알았어? | [오늘 이후로 from this day forward 알았어? Got it?] |

Unit 1

# Review

| Positive (긍정) | Negative (부정) |
|---|---|
| So do I. | Neither do I. |
| 나도 ||

## believe & believe in

배운 내용을 생각하며, 직접 문장을 만들어보세요!

정답확인 : P 242

| 01 | 널 믿고 싶어. |
|----|----|
| 02 | 날 믿어야 돼. 난 진실을 말하는 거야. |
| 03 | 믿기 너무 힘들지? (그렇지?) |
| 04 | 난 그를 믿었어. 내가 정말 바보지. [바보 (such) a fool] |
| 05 | (그거) 믿기 힘들지도 모르지만, 난 그게 정말 좋아. |
| 06 | (너) 그 앨 믿어도 돼. |
| 07 | 모두가 그거 믿을 거야. |
| 08 | 직접 봐야 알지. (내가 그거 보면, 믿을게) |
| 09 | 믿거나 말거나, 그게 진실이야. [믿거나 말거나 believe it or not 진실 the truth] |
| 10 | 그는 나를 안 믿어. |
| 11 | 난 그앨 믿지 않았어.<br>-나도. |
| 12 | 믿기 어려웠어. 내 눈을 의심할 정도였어. (내 눈을 믿을 수 없었어) |
| 13 | 소문이 다는 (사실은) 아니야. (네가 듣는 모든 것을 믿지 마) 사실이 아닐 수도 있어. [사실인 true] |
| 14 | 그 애 말 다 믿으면 안 돼. (그가 말하는 모든 것을 믿어서는 안 돼) |
| 15 | 난 더 이상 뭘 믿을지 모르겠어. |

# Review

| | |
|---|---|
| 16 | 난 그 애가 그 이야기 믿지 않을 것 같아. |
| 17 | 우리 그 애 안 믿는 게 좋을 것 같아. |
| 18 | 아무도 널 믿지 않을 거야. |
| 19 | (너) 날 믿지 않아도 돼. 네가 직접 봐! [직접보다, 확인하다 see for oneself] |
| 20 | 다시는 그 앨 믿지 않을 거야. |
| 21 | 내가 너라면 그 앨 믿지 않을 거야. |
| 22 | 도대체 무슨 말을 하는지 모르겠네. (네가 무슨 말을 하고 있는지 믿을 수가 없어) 제정신이야? (정신 나갔어?) [정신 나간 out of one's mind] |
| 23 | 넌 내 말을 믿지 않을지도 모르지. 하지만 그게 사실이야. |
| 24 | 이제 날 믿겠어? (이제 날 믿니?) |
| 25 | 내가 그 앨 믿어도 될 거 같아? (믿는 게 좋을 것 같아?) |
| 26 | 그게 왜 그렇게 믿기 힘들어? [그렇게 힘든/어려운 so hard] |
| 27 | 널 믿어도 돼? 내가 널 어떻게 믿을 수 있겠어? |
| 28 | 그 앨 믿었니? |
| 29 | 내가 너 말을 왜 믿어야 되는데? (왜 믿는 게 좋을까?) |
| 30 | 그 애가 내 말을 믿을 것 같아? |

## believe & believe in

배운 내용을 생각하며, 직접 문장을 만들어보세요!

| 31 | 난 뭘 믿어야 하지? (뭘 믿는 게 좋을까?) |
|---|---|
| 32 | 그 애 안 와. 믿겨져? (넌 그걸 믿을 수 있어?) |
| 33 | 나 예전엔 신이 있다고 믿었었는데, 더 이상은 아니야. [(존재, 능력) 믿다 believe in] |
| 34 | 그 애는 널 믿어. 그리고 나도. |
| 35 | 난 널 늘 믿었어. 네가 할 수 있을 줄 알았어. |
| 36 | 그는 날 항상 믿었어. 내가 나 자신을 믿지 않을 때조차도. [~때 (조차)도 even when] |
| 37 | 나라면 나 자신을 믿겠어. |
| 38 | 날 믿어줘서 고마워. [고맙다 Thank you for] |
| 39 | 난 예전엔 기적을 믿지 않았었어. 기적은 일어나. [기적 miracles] |
| 40 | 넌 사랑을 믿어? |

## Dialogue Practice

### Agreement

**A:** I enjoyed our time together.
**B:** So did I. We should do it again sometime.

**A:** I can't do this alone.
**B:** Neither can anyone. It's not a one-man job.

**A:** This place is so beautiful.
**B:** Exactly! I was just going to say that.

**A:** He can be so stubborn sometimes.
**B:** You're right. I totally agree with you! / I agree with you 100%.

**A:** It's been hard on all of us.
**B:** Tell me about it!

**A:** I think he's brilliant.
**B:** I couldn't agree more! He's incredible.

## Disagreement

**A:** Everything has to be perfect.
**B:** I don't see it that way. I disagree. Not everything has to be perfect.

**A:** We should strive for perfection.
**B:** I see it differently. Sometimes imperfection is perfection.

**A:** Rich people are happier than average people.
**B:** Not necessarily. That's not always the case.

**A:** It's not the right thing to do!
**B:** Let's agree to disagree.

# Dialogue Practice

### Agreement

**A:** 전 우리가 함께한 시간이 즐거웠어요.
**B:** 저도요. 우리 조만간 또 만나요. (우리 조만간 또 하는 게 좋겠어요)
[조만간 sometime]

**A:** 나 이거 혼자 못하겠어.
**B:** 누구든 마찬가지야. 한 사람이 할 수 있는 일이 아니야. [한 사람이 할 수 있는 일 a one-man job]

**A:** 여기 (이곳) 정말 아름답다.
**B:** 맞아! (정확해) 나 막 그 말 하려고 했는데.

**A:** 그는 가끔 너무 고집이 세. (고집 셀 수 있어) [고집 센 stubborn]
**B:** 네 말이 맞아. (난 너한테) 완전히 동의해! / 난 네 말에 100% 동의해.

**A:** 우리 모두에게 다 힘들었지.(쭉) [힘든 hard on sb, 우리 모두 all of us]
**B:** 내 말이! [그것에 내해 나한테 말해줘!]

**A:** 그는 뛰어난 것 같아. [뛰어난 brilliant]
**B:** 완전 동의해! [더 동의할 수 없어]
그는 대단해.

### Agreement

1. So do I. Etc. [나도]
2. Neither do I. Etc. [나도]
3. Exactly! [맞아! 정확해!]
4. I was going to say that! [그 말 하려고 했어]
5. Youre right. [너 말이 맞아]
6. I (totally) agree with you. [동의해]
7. I agree with you 100%. [100% 동의해]
8. Tell me about it. [내 말이!]
9. I couldn't agree more. [완전/전적 동의해]

### Disagreement

**A:** 모든 게 완벽해야 돼.
**B:** 난 그렇게(그런 식으로) 보지 않아. 난 동의하지 않아. [동의하지 않다 disagree]
　　모든 게 완벽해야 하는 건 아니야. [모든 게 ~ 아니다 not everything]

**A:** (우리) 완벽을 위해 노력해야지. [노력하다 strive for 완벽 perfection]
**B:** 난 다르게 봐. [다르게 differently] 가끔은, 불완벽이 완벽이야. [불완벽, 결함 imperfection]

**A:** 부자인 사람들이 보통 사람들보다 더 행복해.
　　[평균의, 보통의 average]
**B:** 꼭 그런 건 아니야. 항상 그런 건 아니야. (그게 항상 그런 케이스는 아니야)

**A:** 그건(하는 게) 옳은 일이 아니야!
**B:** 의견 차이를 인정하자. (비동의하는 걸로 동의하자) [의견 차이 인정하다 agree to disagree]

#### Disagreement

1. I don't see it that way. [난 그렇게 보지 않아]
2. I disagree. [동의하지 않아]
3. I see it differently. [내 생각은 달라, 난 다르게 봐]
4. Not necessarily! [꼭/반드시 그런 건 아니야]
5. That's not always the case. [항상 그런 건 아니야]
6. Let's agree to disagree. [의견 다름을 인정하자]

# Unit

# 2

상대의 말에
리액션 하고 싶을 때

## Unit 2
### 상대의 말에 리액션 하고 싶을 때

# Do you? "그래? 정말?"

상대의 말에 적절하게 리액션 하는 것은, 대화 안에서 참 많은 역할을 해요. 대화가 끊기지 않고 진행되는 것은 물론, 상대의 이야기에 관심을 표현하여 더 많은 말을 이끌어내기도 하죠. 이럴 때 자주 사용하는 "그래?" "정말?" 이런 표현들을 연습해 볼게요.

| Positive (긍정) | Negative (부정) |
|---|---|
| Do you?<br>Are you?<br>Etc. | Don't you?<br>Aren't you?<br>Etc. |
| 그래? 정말? ||

상대가 한 말에 딱 맞게 리액션 하는 것이라서, 동일한 시제나 조동사를 사용해서 짧게 표현해요. 상대가 과거를 사용해서 이야기하면 동일한 과거로, 현재나 미래 등 다른 시제나 조동사를 사용하면 그것에 맞추어 표현합니다.

> 이렇게 만듭니다!

긍정문에는 동일하게 긍정의 짧은 질문의 형태로,
부정문에는 부정의 질문으로 만들어요.

| Positive (긍정) | Negative (부정) |
|---|---|
| I'm tired.<br>-Are you?<br>I have it.<br>-Do you?<br>I can do it.<br>-Can you? | I'm not tired.<br>-Aren't you?<br>I don't have it.<br>-Don't you?<br>I can't do it.<br>-Can't you? |

<비교>

| Question Tags (3권 8단원) | Conversation Fillers (4권 2단원) |
|---|---|
| 긍정문, **부정 tag.**<br>하지? (그렇지?) | A: 긍정문 -B: **긍정 질문**<br>그래? 정말? |
| 부정문, **긍정 tag.**<br>안 하지? (그렇지?) | A: 부정문 -B: **부정 질문**<br>그래? 정말? |
| You like it, don't you?<br>You don't like it, do you? | I like it. -Do you?<br>I don't like it. -Don't you? |

# Speaking Practice
## 1min

## 긍정문

☞ 오른쪽 힌트를 이용해서, 직접 문장을 만들어보세요!

훈련용 강의 바로 듣기

정답확인 : P 244

| 01 | 너 지금 바쁘면 내가 나중에 다시 전화할 수 있어.<br>- 정말? 고마워. 이따 통화해. (이따 통화할게) | [통화하다 talk to] |
|---|---|---|
| 02 | 내일이면 다 될 거야. 그때 찾으러 와도 돼.<br>- 그래? 잘 됐다. (좋은 소식이다) | [다되는, 준비된 ready] |
| 03 | 너 최소한 6개월마다 비번을 바꿔야 돼.<br>- 그래? | [최소한 at least<br>6개월마다 every six months] |
| 04 | 너를 더 잘 알고 싶어.<br>- 그래? 뭐가 알고 싶은데? | [더 잘 알다/알게 되다<br>get to know sb better] |
| 05 | 그건 걱정하지 마. 내가 너 그거 도와줄게.<br>- 그래? 너밖에 없어. (너가 짱이야) | [짱인, 최고인 the best] |
| 06 | 그건 시간 지나면 괜찮아질 거 같아.<br>-그래? 정말 그랬으면 좋겠다. | [시간이 지나면 괜찮아지다/쉬워지다 get easier with time] |
| 07 | 네가 마음을 정하는 게 좋겠어.<br>- 그래? 근데 내가 뭘 원하는지 모르겠어. | [마음을 정하다, 결정하다<br>make up one's mind] |
| 08 | 너 이거 하는 게 좋을 거 같아.<br>- 정말? 내가 할 수 있을 거 같아? | |
| 09 | 모든 게 괜찮을 거야.<br>- 정말? 확실해? | |
| 10 | 나 지금 나갈 거야.<br>- 그래? 언제 돌아올 거야? | |

## Speaking Practice 1min

## 긍정문

☞ 오른쪽 힌트를 이용해서, 직접 문장을 만들어보세요!

| | | |
|---|---|---|
| 11 | 그거 하려면 돈 많이 들어.<br>-그래? 왜 그렇게 많이 들어?<br>🔊 | [많이 a lot<br>그렇게 많이 so much] |
| 12 | 새로운 환경에 적응하는 데 시간이 좀 걸렸어.<br>-그랬어? 얼마나 걸렸어?<br>🔊 | [시간 좀 a while<br>적응하다 get used to<br>새로운 환경<br>the new environment] |
| 13 | 예전엔 그거 좋아했는데, 더 이상은 아니야.<br>-그래?<br>🔊 | |
| 14 | 쉬울 거야.<br>-그럴까? 그래도 걱정돼. (여전히 걱정돼)<br>🔊 | |
| 15 | 넌 언제든지 와도 돼. (오는 거 환영해)<br>-정말? 정말 고마워.<br>🔊 | [얼마든지/언제든지 해도 돼/<br>환영해<br>You're more than welcome to] |
| 16 | 그 애 엄청 울었어. (울고, 울고, 울었어)<br>-그랬어? 왜 울었어?<br>🔊 | |
| 17 | 이거 가져가도 돼.<br>-그래도 돼? 고마워.<br>🔊 | |
| 18 | 많아. (충분히 있어)<br>-그래?<br>🔊 | [충분히, 많이 plenty] |
| 19 | 나 거기 가봤어.<br>-그래? 언제 거기 가봤어?<br>🔊 | |
| 20 | 나 그때 운전하고 있었어.<br>-그랬어? 어디 가는 길이었어?<br>🔊 | |

Unit 2

# Speaking Practice 1min

## 긍정문

☞ 오른쪽 힌트를 이용해서, 직접 문장을 만들어보세요!

| | | |
|---|---|---|
| 21 | 그건 내게 매우 중요해.<br>- 그래? 왜 그런데? | |
| 22 | 너 정말 잘한다. (정말 재능 있다)<br>- 그래? 그냥 하는 말 아니지, 그렇지? | [잘하는, 재능 있는 talented] |
| 23 | 그 애 그거 잘해.<br>- 정말? 몰랐어. | [잘하는 good/great at] |
| 24 | 나 이거 색깔별로(모든 색) 사고 싶어!<br>-그래? 나도 그러는데. 난 (그게) 맘에 들면 색깔별로 사. | [색깔별로, 모든 색을<br>in every color] |
| 25 | 너 그게 마음에 들면 사지 그래. (사는 게 좋겠어)<br>-그럴까? 정말 그러고 싶어. | |
| 26 | 엄청 추웠어.<br>-그랬어? | [엄청 추운 freezing cold] |
| 27 | 나 그거 하기로 했어.<br>-그랬어? 잘했네 (좋아). 네가 하는 어떤 결정이든 지지해.<br>(네가 하는 모든 결정을 지지해) | [지지하다 support<br>뭐든 whatever<br>결정하다 make a decision] |
| 28 | 나 거기서 일한 지 거의 5년 되어가.<br>-그래? 벌써 5년 됐어? | [거의 almost] |
| 29 | 너한테 말하려고 했어.<br>-그랬어? 언제 (그러려고 했어)? | |
| 30 | 부탁이 있어. (나 도움이 필요해)<br>-그래? 뭔데? 내가 널 위해 뭘 할 수 있어? | [부탁있다 need a favor] |

## Speaking Practice 1min

## 긍정문

☞ 오른쪽 힌트를 이용해서, 직접 문장을 만들어보세요!

| | | |
|---|---|---|
| 31 | 너 잘했어.<br>-그랬어? 고마워. 넌 정말 다정해. | [잘하다 do well/great<br>정말 다정한 so sweet] |
| 32 | 나 그거 이미 알고 있었어.<br>-그랬어? 어떻게 알았어? | [알다, 알게 되다<br>find out] |
| 33 | 우리 정말 재미있었어.<br>-그래? 잘 됐다. (그걸 들으니 기분 좋다) | [재미있다<br>have (so much) fun] |
| 34 | 걔네들 서로 안 지 정말 오래됐어.<br>-정말? | |
| 35 | 거짓말 그만해. 그 애가 내게 모든 걸 말해줬어.<br>-그래? 정확히 뭐라 그랬는데? | [그만하다 stop -ing<br>정확히 exactly] |
| 36 | 그것들은 쓰기 편리해.<br>-그래? | [편리한 convenient ] |
| 37 | 그 애들은 방금 도착했어.<br>-그래? | |
| 38 | 나 너한테 뭐 물어보고 싶었어.<br>-그랬어? 뭔데? (뭐였는데?) | |
| 39 | 네가 어디 있는지 몰랐어. 너에 대해 정말 걱정했잖아.<br>-그랬어? 정말 미안해. | |
| 40 | 나 네가 무슨 말 할 건지 알아.<br>-그래? 내가 무슨 말 할 건데? | |

## Speaking Practice
1min

### 긍정문
☞ 오른쪽 힌트를 이용해서, 직접 문장을 만들어보세요!

| | | |
|---|---|---|
| 41 | 난 내 일이(직업) 좋아.<br>-그래? 뭐가 가장 좋아? (네 일에 관해서 넌 뭐가 가장 좋아?) | [가장 좋아하다 like most] |
| 42 | 복잡했어. 사람 정말 많았어. (많은 사람이 있었어)<br>-그랬어? | [복잡한, 붐비는 crowded] |
| 43 | 나 그거 없앴어.<br>-그랬어? 언제 그랬어? | [없애다 get rid of] |
| 44 | 너한테 뭐 물어보고 싶어.<br>-그래? 뭔데? | |
| 45 | 내가 너한테 손 흔들었는데. (손 흔들고 있었어)<br>-그랬어? 못 봤어. (난 널 보지 않았어) | [손 흔들다 wave at/to sb] |
| 46 | 그거 정말 짜증 났어.<br>-그랬어? 이해해. (공감해) 사람들이 그럴 때 나도 싫더라. | [이해해, 공감해 I feel you.] |
| 47 | 내가 그거 나중에 할게.<br>-그럴래? 고마워. | |
| 48 | 내가 해야 되는 게 (뭔가) 있어서.<br>-그래? 지금 가야 돼? | |
| 49 | 너 와야 돼.<br>-그래? 진짜? (내가 정말 그래야 돼?) | |
| 50 | 내가 그거 하려고 했었는데.<br>-정말? (난 널) 안 믿어. | |

## Speaking Practice — 1min

### 긍정문
☞ 오른쪽 힌트를 이용해서, 직접 문장을 만들어보세요!

| | | |
|---|---|---|
| 51 | 배고파.<br>-그래? 뭐 먹을 거 줄까? (먹을 만한 뭔가를 원해?)<br>🔊 | |
| 52 | 그거 하는 거 깜박했다.<br>-그래? 지금 해도 돼.<br>🔊 | |
| 53 | 그거 정말 스트레스였어. (지금도)<br>-그랬어?<br>🔊 | [스트레스인 stressful] |
| 54 | 미안, 딴생각하느라고. (정신이 다른 데 팔렸어)<br>-그래? 무슨 일 있어? (뭔가 널 신경 쓰게 해?)<br>🔊 | [딴생각하는, 집중 안 되는, 정신 팔린 distracted<br>신경 쓰게 하는 bothering] |
| 55 | 우리 그거 안 하기로 했어.<br>-그랬어? 뭐 할 거야?<br>🔊 | |
| 56 | 그게 예전엔 내가 가장 좋아하는 거였어.<br>-그랬어?<br>🔊 | |
| 57 | 우리 같이 일하고 있어.<br>-정말?<br>🔊 | |
| 58 | 그 애는 로고를 디자인해.<br>-그래?<br>🔊 | |
| 59 | 우리가 그 애를 위해 할 수 있는 게 (뭔가) 있어.<br>-그래? 우리가 뭘 하면 돼? (뭘 할 수 있어?)<br>🔊 | |
| 60 | 나 요즘 운동 좀 했지.<br>-그래? 좋아 보여.<br>🔊 | |

Unit 2

## Speaking Practice 1min

### 부정문

☞ 오른쪽 힌트를 이용해서, 직접 문장을 만들어보세요!

| | | |
|---|---|---|
| 61 | 그거 거기 없어.<br>-그래? 어디 있지? (어디 있는지 궁금하다)<br>🔊 | |
| 62 | 더 이상 뭘 할지 모르겠어. (뭐 다른 걸 할지 모르겠어)<br>-그래? 그렇지. (이해되지)<br>🔊 | [뭐 다른 거 더 what else<br>이해되는, 정상적인, 자연스러운 understandable] |
| 63 | (그거) 상관없어.<br>-그래? 확실해?<br>🔊 | [상관있다, 중요하다 matter] |
| 64 | 그거 여기 없던데.<br>-그랬어? 어디 갔지?<br>🔊 | |
| 65 | 나 거기 아직 안 가봤어.<br>-그랬어?<br>🔊 | |
| 66 | 나 그거 못했어.<br>-그래? 그럼 언제 할 수 있어?<br>🔊 | |
| 67 | 너 오는 줄 몰랐네. (난 널 기대하고 있지 않았어)<br>-그랬어? 어제 너한테 말했잖아.<br>🔊 | [기대하다 expect] |
| 68 | 그 애 이거 안 좋아해.<br>-정말?<br>🔊 | |
| 69 | 너 그거 안 해도 돼.<br>-진짜?<br>🔊 | |
| 70 | 모자랐어. (충분하지 않았어)<br>-그랬어?<br>🔊 | |

# Speaking Practice
## 1min

**부정문**

☞ 오른쪽 힌트를 이용해서, 직접 문장을 만들어보세요!

| | | |
|---|---|---|
| 71 | 너 그거 안 좋아할 거야.<br>-그럴까? | |
| 72 | 듣고 있지 않았어. (집중하고 있지 않았어)<br>-그랬어? 무슨 생각하고 있었어? | [집중하다, 듣다, 보다 pay attention] |
| 73 | 그거 안전해 보이지 않아.<br>-그런가? | |
| 74 | 며칠 동안 잠을 잘 못 잤어.<br>-그랬어? | |
| 75 | 그거 안 아팠어.<br>-그랬어? | [아프다 hurt] |
| 76 | 우리 그거 안 가져가는 게 좋겠어.<br>-그런가? | |
| 77 | 그 애 안 올 것 같아.<br>-그래? 그 애 바빠? | |
| 78 | 나 그거 안 가져왔어.<br>-그래? 걱정 마. 내가 (그거 너한테) 빌려줄게. | |
| 79 | 나 아무것도 안 했어.<br>-그랬어? | |
| 80 | 우리 아직 나가면 안 돼.<br>-그래? 언제 나가도 돼? | |

## Speaking Practice 1min

**부정문**

☞ 오른쪽 힌트를 이용해서, 직접 문장을 만들어보세요!

| | | |
|---|---|---|
| 81 | 나 지금 집에 안 가.<br>-그래? 어디 가? | |
| 82 | 그거 거기 없을걸.<br>-그러려나? 어디 있는 거 같아? | |
| 83 | 나 거기 안 가려고 했었어.<br>-그랬어? 왜 갔었어? | |
| 84 | 너에게 상처 줄 의도가 아니었어.<br>-그래? 알아. | [진심/의도/의미이다 mean to<br>상처 주다, 아프게 하다 hurt] |
| 85 | 난 그거 그렇게 어려울 거 같지 않아.<br>-그래? (나) 다행이다. | [다행인, 안심인 relieved ] |
| 86 | 네가 걱정해야 되는 거 아무것도 없어.<br>-정말? 그랬으면 좋겠다. (너 말이 맞으면 좋겠다) | [~면 좋겠다, 희망하다 hope] |
| 87 | 아직 잔돈을 제게 주시지 않으셨어요.<br>-그래요? 죄송해요. | |
| 88 | 그건 네 잘못이 아니었어.<br>-그런가? 안 그런 거 같아. (그게 그렇게 느껴지지 않아) | [그렇게 like it] |
| 89 | 나 어렸을 땐 이거 안 좋아했었는데.<br>-그랬어? | |
| 90 | 나라면 그렇게 말 안 해.<br>-그래? 뭐라고 하겠어? | |

## Speaking Practice 1min

### 부정문

☞ 오른쪽 힌트를 이용해서, 직접 문장을 만들어보세요!

| | | |
|---|---|---|
| 91 | 지금 취소 안 돼. (너 지금 취소 못해)<br>-그래요? | |
| 92 | 여기 사람 많이 없다.<br>-그래? 몇 명 있어? | |
| 93 | 그 애를 확신시키는 건 쉽지 않았어.<br>-그랬어? | [확신시키다 convince] |
| 94 | 우리 그거 안 가져가는 게 좋겠어.<br>-그럴까? | |
| 95 | 너 아무 잘못하지 않았어.<br>-그래? | [아무 잘못<br>anything wrong] |
| 96 | 그거 오래되지 않았어.<br>-그래? 오래된 거 같아. (그건 영원한 느낌이야) | [~느낌이다 feel like] |
| 97 | 난 부끄럽지 않아.<br>-그래? 당연히 안 그래야지. (어쨌든 넌 안 그런 게 좋겠어) | [부끄러운, 창피한 ashamed<br>어쨌든 anyway] |
| 98 | 나라면 그거 안 해.<br>-그래? 넌 뭘 하겠어? | |
| 99 | 그 애는 나한테 아무 말도 안 했어.<br>-그랬어? 그럼, 어떻게 알았어? | |
| 100 | 나 지금 뭘 해야 될지 모르겠어.<br>-그래? | |

Unit 2

# Review

복습 강의 바로 듣기

| Positive (긍정) | Negative (부정) |
| --- | --- |
| So do I. | Neither do I. |
| 나도 ||
| Do you? | Don't you? |
| 그래? 정말? ||

## know & a know-it-all

배운 내용을 생각하며, 직접 문장을 만들어보세요!

정답확인 : P 249

| 01 | 너는 알아야 돼. |
|---|---|
| 02 | 너에 대해 다 (모든 걸) 알고 싶어. |
| 03 | 그 애는 알지도 몰라. |
| 04 | 그럴 줄 알았어. (난 그걸 알았어) 난 그런 일이 일어날 줄 알았어.<br>-그랬어? |
| 05 | 예전엔 그 애에 대해서 모든 걸 알았었는데. 우리 예전엔 정말 가까웠었어.<br>[정말 가까운 so close] |
| 06 | 그 애는 다 알고 있어. (모든 것에 대해 알아) |
| 07 | 모두가 알 거야. 난 그걸 원하지 않아. |
| 08 | (나 그거) **안 지 좀 됐어.** [좀 for a while]<br>-그래? 어떻게 알았어? [알다, 알게 되다 find out] |
| 09 | 아니야. 나도 그 정도는 알아야지. (그 정도는 아는 게 좋겠어)<br>[그 정도는 알아, 안 해야 되는 거 알아 know better] |
| 10 | 아니, 난 그거 안 할 거야. 그 정도로 어리석지는 않아.<br>[그 정도는 알다, 그럴 정도로 어리석지 않다 know better] |
| 11 | 보면 알 거야. (너 그거 보면 넌 그걸 알 거야)<br>-그럴까? |
| 12 | 확실히 알 수 있는 방법이 없어. [확실히 알다 know for sure] |
| 13 | 꿀팁이다. (알아서 좋아) 내게 말해줘서 고마워. |
| 14 | 넌 날 정말 잘 알아, 그렇지? [정말 잘 so well] |
| 15 | 그 애는 알걸. |

# Review

| | |
|---|---|
| 16 | **나라면 알 거야.** |
| 17 | **궁금해 죽겠어.** (알고 싶어 죽겠어) [하고 싶어 죽겠다, 정말 하고 싶다 be dying to] |
| 18 | **눈 깜짝할 새에 끝날 거야.** (그건 끝날 거야 네가 그걸 알기도 전에)<br>[끝인 over 눈 깜짝할 새, 순식간에 before you know it] |
| 19 | **내가 알기로는, 문제없어.** [내가 아는 한, 알기로는 as far as I know] |
| 20 | **알고 싶지 않아.** |
| 21 | **그 앤 아무것도 모르지?** |
| 22 | **그건 몰랐어.** (그거에 대해서는 몰랐어)<br>-그랬니? |
| 23 | **그 앤 이거 몰라야 돼.** (그 앤 이거에 대해 알면 안 돼) |
| 24 | **그 앤 몰라도 돼.** |
| 25 | **나라면 뭘 할지 모를 거야.** |
| 26 | **(우리) 확실히 알 수는 없어.** |
| 27 | **너 없이 어떡할지 모르겠어.** (너 없이 내가 뭘 할 건지 모르겠어) |
| 28 | **아무도 모를걸.** |
| 29 | **그 애들은 아직 아무것도 모를지도 몰라.** |
| 30 | **가끔은 모르는 게 아는 것보다 나아.** [모르는 것 not knowing 아는 것 knowing] |

## know & a know-it-all

배운 내용을 생각하며, 직접 문장을 만들어보세요!

| | |
|---|---|
| 31 | 아는 게 모르는 것보다 나은가? 어떻게 생각해? |
| 32 | 뭐가 알고 싶어? |
| 33 | 뭘 알고 있어? 얼마나 알고 있어? |
| 34 | 너희 서로 안 지 얼마나 됐어? |
| 35 | 이거(에 대해) 알고 있었니? |
| 36 | 제가 어떻게 확실히 알 수 있죠? |
| 37 | (내가) 알아야 돼? |
| 38 | 그 애가 알 거 같아? |
| 39 | 우리는 언제쯤 확실히 알 수 있어요? |
| 40 | **차에 대해 좀 아니?** [좀/많이 알다 know much (about)] |
| 41 | 그 애는 정말 아는 체해. (정말 잘난척하는 애야)<br>[아는 체/잘난척하는 사람 (such) a know-it-all] |
| 42 | 귀여운 잘난 척쟁이! (넌 작은 잘난척쟁이지, 그렇지?) |
| 43 | 그 애 예전엔 잘 난척했었어. |
| 44 | 나 잘난 척하는 사람 아니야. |
| 45 | 사람들은 아는 척하는 사람들을 좋아하지 않아. |

Unit 2

## Dialogue Practice

**Conversation fillers**

**A**: You have so much potential.

**B**: Do I?


**A**: I don't have Instagram. I'm not on social media.

**B**: Aren't you? Why is that?


**A**: I think it's too late.

**B**: Well. Actually, that is true.


**A**: I give up. I don't want to do it anymore.

**B**: You're kidding! Are you serious?


**A**: I can't come to the gathering.

**B**: What a pity! It wouldn't be the same without you.

**A**: We have to change the venue.

**B**: What a shame! I was looking forward to going there.

**A**: He was in a car accident.

**B**: Oh, no! How awful!

**A**: It was so sad.

**B**: Kind of. / Sort of.

# Dialogue Practice

**Conversation fillers**

**A**: 넌 정말 많은 잠재력이 있어. [잠재력 (so much) potential]

**B**: 그래?


**A**: 난 인스타그램 없어. SNS 안 해. [sns 하는 on social media]

**B**: 그래? 왜?


**A**: 너무 늦은 것 같아.

**B**: 음. 사실, 그게 맞네. (그게 사실이야) [사실은 actually, 사실인 true]


**A**: 난 포기(해). 더 이상 이거 하기 싫어.

**B**: (설마) 농담이지! (너 농담하는 거지) 진짜야? (심각해?)


**A**: 나 모임에 못 가. (모임에 못 와) [모임 the gathering]

**B**: 아쉽다! 너 없이는 같지 않을 거야.

**A**: 우리 장소를 바꿔야 돼. [장소 the venue]

**B**: 안타깝다! 거기 가는 거 기대하고 있었는데. [기대/고대하다 look forward to -ing]

**A**: 그는 교통사고가 났어. [교통사고 난 in a car accident]

**B**: 안 돼! 세상에! (끔찍해라)

**A**: 정말 슬펐어.

**B**: 좀 그랬지.
[좀 그렇지, 그렇기도 하지 kind of/sort of]

### Conversation fillers

1. Do you? Don't you? etc. [그래?]
2. Well. [음, 글쎄]
3. Actually, [사실은,]
4. You're joking/kidding!
   [설마 농담이지]
5. What a pity. (That's a pity.)
   [아쉽다, 안됐다]
6. What a shame. (That's a shame.)
   [안타깝다, 아깝다]
7. How awful! How terrible!
   [세상에! 어머나! 끔찍해라!]
8. Kind of. / Sort of.
   [쫌 그렇지, 그렇기도 하지]

# Unit

# 3

주인공을 물어보는
질문을 하고 싶을 때

## Unit 3
### 주인공을 물어보는 질문을 하고 싶을 때

# Subject Questions "누가? 뭐가?"

저희가 지금까지 주로 연습한 질문들은, 주인공을 따로 넣어주었어요. 그래서, 그 주인공이 "무엇을" 하는지, 혹은 "누구를" 만나는지 등의 **의문사가 목적어**인 문장들이었는데요. 이번 단원에서는 그 **의문사 자체가 "주인공"**인 질문들을 연습해 볼게요.

| Subject Questions |
|---|
| Who 동사? <br> What 동사? |
| 누가? <br> 뭐가? |

### 이렇게 만듭니다!

의문사로 사용한 Who, 혹은 What 자체가 주인공이라서
적절한 **동사를 바로 사용**하면 돼요!

| | |
|---|---|
| What happened? | Who came? |
| What's happening? | Who's coming? |
| What's happened? | Who's come? |
| What's going to happen? | Who's going to come? |

<주의>

의문사를 **"단수 취급"** 하므로 be 동사나, 현재형들에서는 조심해야 돼요!

Who is doing this? (O)    Who are doing this? (X)
Who do this? (X)    Who does this? (O)

<비교>

| Object Questions | Subject Questions |
|---|---|
| Who did you hit?<br>너 **누구** 때렸어? | Who hit you?<br>**누가** 널 때렸어? |
| What did you change?<br>너 **뭘** 바꿨어? | What changed?<br>**뭐가** 바뀌었어? |

# Speaking Practice
## 1min

☞ 오른쪽 힌트를 이용해서, 직접 문장을 만들어보세요!

정답확인 : P 250

| 01 | 누가 알아?<br>너 운이 좋을 수도 있어. | |
|---|---|---|
| 02 | 누가 알았겠어?<br>그건 완전히 예상 밖이었어. | [예상 밖인, 기대 못한 unexpected] |
| 03 | 이거 누가 줬어?<br>너 이거 어디서 났어? | |
| 04 | 이거 누가 그랬어?<br>누가 했는지 너 알아? | |
| 05 | 누가 이러는 거야?<br>(누가 이걸 하는 거야?) | |
| 06 | 그걸 누가 하겠어?<br>아무도 안 할 거야. | |
| 07 | 누가 그런 짓을 하겠어? | [그런 짓 such a thing] |
| 08 | 누가 그래?<br>(누가 그렇게 말했어?) | |
| 09 | 누가 너한테 그 말 했어?<br>그건 사실이 아니야. | |
| 10 | 누가 너한테 그 질문했어?<br>누가 그랬는지 기억나? | |

# Speaking Practice
**1min**

☞ 오른쪽 힌트를 이용해서, 직접 문장을 만들어보세요!

| 11 | 누가 전화했어? | |
|---|---|---|
| 12 | 누가 이 시간에 너한테 전화하는 거야? | [이 시간에 at this hour] |
| 13 | 누가 그 애한테 전화할까?<br>그에게는 아무도 없어. | |
| 14 | 누가 그걸 싫어해?<br>모두 다 그거 좋아하잖아. | |
| 15 | 이거 누가 찾았어?<br>누가 이거 찾은 건지 말해줄래? | |
| 16 | 이거 누가 깼어?<br>누가 이거 깼는지 봤어? | |
| 17 | 누가 내 책 가져갔지? | |
| 18 | 누가 너 거기 데려갈 거야?<br>내가 태워다 줄까? | [데려가다 take sb<br>태워주다 give sb a ride] |
| 19 | 파티에 누가 와?<br>몇 명이 와? | |
| 20 | 내가 밖에 있는 동안에, 누군가 여기 왔었어?<br>누가 왔었어? | |

Unit 3

# Speaking Practice 1min

☞ 오른쪽 힌트를 이용해서, 직접 문장을 만들어보세요!

| 21 | 무슨 일이야? (지금)<br>왜 모두 여기 있어?<br>🔊 | [일이 일어나다, 벌어지다<br>go on] |
|---|---|---|
| 22 | 문제가 뭐였어?<br>🔊 | |
| 23 | 무슨 일이야?<br>(뭐가 문제야?)<br>🔊 | [문제 matter] |
| 24 | 뭐가 잘못됐어?<br>난 그게 어디서 잘못된 건지 알고 싶어.<br>🔊 | [잘못되다 go wrong] |
| 25 | 네 폰에 문제 있어?<br>그거 뭐가 문제야?(뭐가 잘못됐어?)<br>🔊 | [문제 있다<br>have a problem with<br>문제인, 잘못된 wrong with] |
| 26 | 그거 지금 돼?<br>뭐가 문제였어?(뭐가 잘못됐었어?)<br>🔊 | |
| 27 | 뭐가 문제 같아?<br>(뭐가 문제처럼 보여?)<br>🔊 | [~처럼 보이다 seem to] |
| 28 | 그 안에 뭐 있어?<br>🔊 | |
| 29 | 거기 안에 뭔가 있었어?<br>그 안에 뭐 있었어?<br>🔊 | |
| 30 | 뭐가 바뀌었어?<br>뭐가 네 마음을 바꿨어?<br>🔊 | |

# Speaking Practice
**1min**

☞ 오른쪽 힌트를 이용해서, 직접 문장을 만들어보세요!

| | | |
|---|---|---|
| 31 | 그 애한테 무슨 일이 생길까? | [~일이 생기다, 일어나다 happen to] |
| 32 | 그 애 어떻게 된 거야? (그 애한테 무슨 일이 생긴 거야?)<br>그 애 지난주에 떠난 후로, 아무도 소식을 못 들었어. | [소식을 듣다 hear from] |
| 33 | 아까 너 어떻게 된 거야?<br>(아까 너한테 무슨 일이 생긴 거야?) | [아까 earlier] |
| 34 | 너 입술이 왜 그래?<br>(너의 입술한테 무슨 일이 생긴 거야?) | |
| 35 | 나한테 이게 무슨 일이야? (지금 내게 무슨 일이 일어나고 있는 거야?)<br>모든 게 너무 빠르게 일어나고 있어. | |
| 36 | 어쩐 일이야? (뭐가 널 여기로 보냈어?)<br>나 여기서 전에 너 본 적이 없는데. | |
| 37 | 어쩐 일로 왔어?<br>(뭐가 널 여기로 보냈어?) | |
| 38 | 여기 안에 연기 많이 나네.<br>뭐가 타는 거지? | [연기 많이 나는 smoky] |
| 39 | 네 코에 있는 게 뭐야? | |
| 40 | 너 왜 이렇게 오래 걸렸어? (너 뭐가 이렇게 오래 걸렸어?)<br>이 긴 세월 어디 갔다 왔어? 평생 너를 기다렸어. | [이 긴 세월 all these years<br>평생 all one's life] |

Unit 3

☞ 오른쪽 힌트를 이용해서, 직접 문장을 만들어보세요!

| 41 | 여기 안에 누가 이걸 가져다 뒀어?<br>여기 안에 아무것도 두면 안 돼.<br>🔊 | |
|---|---|---|
| 42 | 누군가 널 봤어?<br>누가 널 봤어?<br>🔊 | |
| 43 | 누가 그럴 시간이 있어?<br>그건 시간 낭비야.<br>🔊 | [~시간 time for<br>시간 낭비 a waste of time] |
| 44 | 누가 그걸 할 시간이 있었겠어?<br>시간 없었어.<br>🔊 | [~할 시간 time to] |
| 45 | 누가 그랬어? (이거 너한테 누가 했어?)<br>누가 널 때렸어?<br>🔊 | |
| 46 | 누가 게임 이겼어?<br>누가 승자였어?<br>🔊 | [승자 the winner] |
| 47 | 이것들 누가 만들었어?<br>🔊 | |
| 48 | 누가 이걸 여기다 놨어?<br>너야? (너였어?)<br>🔊 | |
| 49 | 그걸 누가 너한테 가르쳐 줬어?<br>독학했어? (그거 독학이었어?)<br>🔊 | [독학인, 스스로 배운<br>self-taught] |
| 50 | 누가 너한테 이걸 보냈어?<br>누가 했는지 알아?<br>🔊 | |

68　　　　　　　　　　　　　　　　　　　기초영어 1000문장 말하기 연습 4

☞ 오른쪽 힌트를 이용해서, 직접 문장을 만들어보세요!

| | | |
|---|---|---|
| 51 | 뭐가 널 슬프게 해?<br>(뭐가 널 슬프게 만들어?) | [슬프게 하다 make-sad] |
| 52 | 뭐가 널 울게 했어?<br>(뭐가 널 울게 만들었어?) | |
| 53 | 왜 그렇게 말해?<br>(뭐가 널 그렇게 말하게 만들어?) | |
| 54 | 왜 그렇게 생각해? (뭐가 널 그렇게 생각하게 만들어?)<br>그게 날 슬프게 한다. (슬프게 만들어) | |
| 55 | 왜 마음 바꿨어?<br>(뭐가 네 마음을 바꾸게 만들었어?) | |
| 56 | 뭐가 널 행복하게 만들어?<br>널 행복하게 만드는 5가지를 말해줄래? | [5가지 5 things] |
| 57 | 왜 그렇게 확신해?<br>(뭐가 널 그렇게 확신하게 만들어?) | [그렇게 확신하는<br>so sure] |
| 58 | 이게 다(모두) 뭐야? 어쩐 일이야? | [어쩐 일이야? 무슨 일이야?<br>What gives?] |
| 59 | 왜 그런 생각을 하게 됐어?<br>(뭐가 너한테 그 아이디어를 줬어?) | |
| 60 | 왜 그런 느낌을 가졌어?<br>(뭐가 너한테 그 인상을 줬어?) | [인상 impression] |

Unit 3

# Speaking Practice
## 1min

☞ 오른쪽 힌트를 이용해서, 직접 문장을 만들어보세요!

| 61 | 너한테 그걸 누가 팔았어? | |
| --- | --- | --- |
| 62 | 누군가 여기 있어요?<br>거기 누구예요? | |
| 63 | 나 아무한테도 말 안 했어.<br>-나도. 그럼, 누가 했지? | |
| 64 | 누가 그런 걸 해?<br>말도 안 돼. (그건 말로 표현할 수 없어) | [말로 표현할 수 없는<br>unspeakable] |
| 65 | 누가 내 케이크 먹었어? | |
| 66 | 그걸 누가 좋아해?<br>아무도 안 좋아해. | |
| 67 | 그런 걸 누가 원하겠어? | |
| 68 | 나랑 누가 데이트하고 싶겠어?<br>나 매력 없는 느낌이야. | [데이트하다 go out with<br>매력 없는 unattractive] |
| 69 | 너랑 누가 병원에 같이 갔어?<br>너 혼자 가지 않았지? | |
| 70 | 이거 누가 시켰어?<br>이거 누구 거야? | |

# Speaking Practice 1min

☞ 오른쪽 힌트를 이용해서, 직접 문장을 만들어보세요.

| | | |
|---|---|---|
| 71 | 어느 거였어? 빨간 거였어? | [빨간 거 the red one] |
| 72 | 어느 게 더 돈 많이 들어? | |
| 73 | 어느 게 시간이 덜 들까? | [더 적은 시간, 시간이 덜 less time] |
| 74 | 어느 부분이 가장 좋았어? | [가장 좋은, 마음에 드는 one's favorite] |
| 75 | 네가 지금까지 본 것 중에 최고의 영화가 뭐야? | [지금까지 ever ] |
| 76 | 뭐가 사고 원인이 되었어? | [원인이 되다, 초래하다 cause] |
| 77 | 그 컨퍼런스에 몇 명 왔어? | |
| 78 | 세미나에 몇 명 참석할까? | |
| 79 | 몇 명이 새 서비스로 전환했어? | [바꾸다, 전환하다 switch to] |
| 80 | 누가 신경 써?<br>아무도 신경 안 써 | [신경 쓰다 give a shit/crap, care] |

# Speaking Practice 1min

☞ 오른쪽 힌트를 이용해서, 직접 문장을 만들어보세요!

| 81 | 누가 그거 고치고 있어? | |
|---|---|---|
| 82 | 누가 내 물건 썼어? (사용) | |
| 83 | 이거 누가 썼어? (글씨)<br>네가 이거 쓴 거야? | |
| 84 | 누가 너한테 그런 조언했어?<br>현명한 조언이다. | [조언하다 give-advice] |
| 85 | 누가 저 집에 살아? | |
| 86 | 예전에 저 집에 누가 살았었는지는 모르지만,<br>지금 누가 살고 있는지는 알아. | |
| 87 | 이거 누구 책임이야?<br>그게 누구의 책임인데? | [책임인 responsible for<br>책임 responsibility] |
| 88 | 누가 널 믿을까?<br>(누가 널 믿을 거야?) | |
| 89 | 네 인생에서 네게 일어난 것 중 가장 최고의 일이 뭐야? | [가장 최고의 일<br>the best thing] |
| 90 | 뭐가 걸려? (뭐가 널 막고 있어?)<br>너 왜 결정을 힘들어해? | [결정이 힘든, 망설이는<br>indecisive] |

# Speaking Practice 1min

☞ 오른쪽 힌트를 이용해서, 직접 문장을 만들어보세요!

| 91 | 어떤 종류의 직업이 네 관심을 끌어? | [어떤 종류의 직업 what kind of jobs 관심 끌다, 흥미롭다 interest] |
|---|---|---|
| 92 | 네가 그걸 하도록 감명을 준 건 누구야? | [영감 주다, 감명 주다 inspire] |
| 93 | 이거 좋아하는 사람?<br>(누가 이걸 좋아해?) | |
| 94 | 펜 있는 사람?<br>(누가 펜 가지고 있어?) | |
| 95 | 답 아는 사람?<br>(누가 그 답을 알아?) | |
| 96 | 뭐 먹을 사람?<br>(뭔가 먹고 싶은 사람 누구야?) | |
| 97 | 와인 좋아하는 사람?<br>(누가 와인 좋아해?) | |
| 98 | 내 팀 하고 싶은 사람?<br>(누가 내 팀 하고 싶어?) | [내 팀 on my team] |
| 99 | 부자 되고 싶은 사람?<br>(누가 백만장자 되고 싶어?) | |
| 100 | 핸드폰 터지는 사람?<br>(누구의 폰이 아직도 신호가 있어?) | [(폰) 터지다, 신호가 있다 have a signal] |

Unit 3

# Review

복습 강의 바로 듣기

| Positive (긍정) | Negative (부정) | Question |
|---|---|---|
| So do I. | Neither do I. | - |
| 나도 | | - |
| Do you? | Don't you? | - |
| 그래? 정말? | | - |
| - | - | Who 동사? What 동사? |
| - | - | 누가? 뭐가? |

## come & come with

배운 내용을 생각하며, 직접 문장을 만들어보세요!

정답확인 : P 253

| 01 | 우리 예전엔 여기 매일 왔었는데. 우리가 가장 좋아하는 장소였어. [곳, 장소 spot] |
|---|---|
| 02 | 그는 여기 매주 금요일마다 와. <br> -그래? |
| 03 | 난 여기 5분 전에 왔어. 여기 온 지 5분 됐어. |
| 04 | 너 와야 돼. 우리 같이 좋은 시간 보낼 거야. |
| 05 | 너 시간 있으면 와도 돼. |
| 06 | 나 여기 전에 여러 번 와봤어. |
| 07 | 그 애가 올 거 같아. |
| 08 | 너도 오는 게 좋을 것 같아. |
| 09 | 그 애는 집에 오고 있었어. |
| 10 | 그 애가 올 수도 있어. 모르겠어. |
| 11 | 그 애가 오고 있어. 곧 여기 올 거야. (금방 여기 있을 거야) |
| 12 | 난 오려고 했었는데, 못 왔어. |
| 13 | 나는 여기 다닌 지 6개월 됐어. |
| 14 | 너도 오지 그래. (너도 오지 뭐) |
| 15 | 너도 오고 싶지? (그렇지?) |

# Review

| | |
|---|---|
| 16 | 나는 늘 여기 와보고 싶었어.<br>-나도. |
| 17 | **와서 뽀뽀해 줘, 응?** [뽀뽀하다, 키스하다 give sb a kiss] |
| 18 | 그 앤 오지 않는 게 좋을 것 같아. |
| 19 | 그 애가 올지 모르겠어. |
| 20 | 여기 안 와본 지 정말 오래됐다. [정말 오래 for ages] |
| 21 | 너 오기 싫었지? |
| 22 | (너) 싫으면 오지 않아도 돼. |
| 23 | 난 그 애 안 올 것 같아.<br>-정말? |
| 24 | 미안, 어제 네 파티에 못 가서. |
| 25 | 그 애들은 안 올지도 몰라. |
| 26 | 나라도 여기 안 와. |
| 27 | 여기 다시는 오지 마. |
| 28 | 그 앤 오지 않으려고 했었어.<br>-그랬어? |
| 29 | 성공은 쉽게 오지 않아. 쉽게 오는 것은 쉽게 가.<br>[쉽게 오다 come easy 쉽게 얻는 건 쉽게 잃는다. Easy come, easy go.] |
| 30 | 그 앤 오면 안 돼. 보고 싶지 않아. |

## come & come with

배운 내용을 생각하며, 직접 문장을 만들어보세요!

| | |
|---|---|
| 31 | 그 앤 안 올 거지, 그렇지? |
| 32 | 그건 내게 쉽지 않았어. (자연스럽게 오지 않았어) 그걸 위해 노력해야 했어.<br>[쉽다, 자연스럽게 하다 come naturally to sb 노력하다 work hard for] |
| 33 | 내가 왜 여기 왔는지 모르겠어. |
| 34 | 언제 왔어? |
| 35 | 여기 온 지 얼마나 됐어? |
| 36 | 몇 시에 올래? |
| 37 | 내가 언제 와야 돼? |
| 38 | 너 언제 올 것 같은데? |
| 39 | 그 앤 여기 얼마나 자주 와? |
| 40 | 내가 몇 시에 갈까? |
| 41 | 엄마도 와? (오고 있어?) |
| 42 | 나도 가도 돼? |
| 43 | 내가 언제 가는 게 좋을 것 같아? |
| 44 | 누가 오겠어? (누가 올 거야?) |
| 45 | 그건 선물백이 같이 나와. [선물백 a gift bag] |
| 46 | 그 요리는 샐러드가 나와요. [그 요리/음식/메뉴 the dish] |
| 47 | 이거 스프랑 같이 나왔어. |
| 48 | 그거 감자튀김이랑 같이 나오나요? |

## Dialogue Practice

**Riddles**

**Q**: How many months have 28 days?

**A**: All 12 months. Every month has 28 days.

**Q**: What has legs, but doesn't walk?

**A**: A table. And a chair. They have legs, but don't walk.

**Q**: What building has most stories?

**A**: The library. The Lotte World Tower has 123 stories. But the library has more stories!

**Q**: What kind of lion never roars?

**A**: A dandelion. A dandelion is a plant. It doesn't make any sound, let alone roar.

**Q**: What can you catch, but never throw?

**A**: A cold. You can catch a cold, but you can never throw a cold.

**Q**: What's always coming, but never arrives?

**A**: Tomorrow. The next day is always tomorrow. When tomorrow arrives, it is today.


**Q**: What is always in front of you, but you can't see it?

**A**: The future. The future is always in front of us, but it's impossible to see. We can make plans about the future, but we can't see it until it becomes the present.


**Q**: If you drop me, I will crack. If you smile at me, I'll smile back. What am I?

**A**: a mirror.


**Q**: Poor people have it. Rich people need it. If you eat it, you die. What is it?

**A**: Nothing. Poor people have nothing. Rich people need nothing. And if you eat nothing, you die.

# Dialogue Practice

**Riddles**

**Q**: 28일을 가지고 있는 달은 몇 개일까? (몇 개의 달이 28일을 가지고 있나?)

**A**: 12 달 모두. 모든 달이 28일을 가지고 있다.


**Q**: 다리는 있는데, 걷지 않는 것은? (뭐가 다리를 가지고 있고, 걷지는 않을까?)

**A**: 테이블. 의자. (그들) 다리는 있지만, 걷지는 않는다.


**Q**: 가장 많은 이야기를 가진 빌딩은?
   (무슨 빌딩이 가장 많은 이야기를 가지고 있을까?) [가장 많은 이야기 most stories]

**A**: 도서관. 롯데월드 타워는 123층(stories) 을 가지고 있다.
   하지만 도서관이 더 많은 이야기(stories)를 가지고 있다! [층 stories]


**Q**: 포효하지 않는 사자(lion)는?
   (어떤 종류의 사자가 절대 포효하지 않을까?) [포효하다 roar]

**A**: 민들레. (A dandelion)  민들레는 식물이다.
   (그것은) 아무 소리를 내지 않는다, 포효는 고사하고.
   [소리 내다 make sound ~커녕, 고사하고 let alone]


**Q**: 잡을 수(catch)는 있는데, 절대 던질 수는 없는 것은?
   (네가 잡을 수는 있지만, 절대 던질 수는 없는 것은 무엇일까?)

**A**: 감기. (A cold)
   (너) 감기는 걸릴 수 있지만, 절대 감기를 던질 수는 없다.
   [감기 걸리다 catch a cold]

**Q**: 항상 오고 있는데, 결코 도착하지 않는 것은?
　　(무엇이 항상 오고 있지만, 절대 도착하지 않을까?)

**A**: 내일. 다음날이 항상 내일이다. [다음날 the next day]
　　내일이 도착하면, 오늘이다.


**Q**: 항상 네 앞에 있는데, (네가) 볼 수 없는 것은?
　　(무엇이 항상 네 앞에 있지만, 넌 그걸 볼 수 없을까?) [앞에 in front of]

**A**: 미래. (The future)
　　미래는 항상 우리 앞에 있지만, 보는 게 불가능하다.
　　우리는 미래에 대한 계획을 세울 수 있지만,
　　(우리는) 그것을 볼 수 없다. 그것이 현재가 될 때까지.
　　[계획 세우다 make plans 되다 become 현재 the present]


**Q**: (네가) 날 떨어뜨리면, 나는 깨질 거야. [깨지다, 갈라지다 crack]
　　(네가) 나에게 미소 지으면, 나도 미소 지을 거야.
　　[미소 짓다 smile at ~도 미소 짓다, 미소로 답하다 smile back] 난 뭘까?

**A**: 거울.


**Q**: 가난한 사람들은 이걸 가지고 있어. 부자 사람들은 이게 필요해.
　　(네가) 이걸 먹으면, 넌 죽어. 이게 뭘까?

**A**: 아무것도 아니야. (Nothing)
　　가난한 사람들은 아무것도 없어. 부자는 아무것도 필요 없어.
　　그리고 네가 아무것도 안 먹으면, 넌 죽어.

# Unit

# 4

확인을 위해서
부정의 질문을 하고 싶을 때

# Unit 4

## 확인을 위해서 부정의 질문을 하고 싶을 때

# Don't you? "안 해?"

한국말과 마찬가지로 영어에서도, 무언가 예상 밖이라 재확인하거나, 내가 알고 있는 것을 확인하기 위해서 부정의 형태로 질문을 합니다. 이외에도 부정의 질문은, 놀라움을 표현할 수 있고, 상대의 동의를 얻기도 쉬워서 처음 대화를 시작하기 좋은 표현들로 사용하기도 해요.

| Negative Questions | | |
|---|---|---|
| Don't you?<br>Aren't you?<br>Etc. | Do you not?<br>Are you not?<br>Etc. | Why don't you? |
| 안 해? || 하는 게 어때? |

부정의 형태로 질문하는 방법은 짧게 축약형으로 하는데요. 줄이지 않고 길게 할 때는 주인공을 사이에 넣어서 순서가 좀 달라요.

또한, "Why don't you?" 를 사용하는 문장은 "하는 게 어때?"로 무언가를 제안할 때도 사용할 수 있어요!

**<Why don't you/I/we?>**

Why don't we do this together? 우리 이거 같이 하는 게 어때?
Why don't you stay here? 너 여기에 있는 게 어때?

> 이렇게 만듭니다!

의문의 문장에서, 적절한 시제나 조동사의 부정 축약의 형태로 만들어요! 축약하지 않고 길게 나열할 때는 조금 더 강렬해서 비판이나 짜증의 느낌이 들어가기도 해요.

| Don't you like it? | Do you not like it? |
|---|---|
| Didn't you do it? | Did you not do it? |

<주의>
부정 질문에 대답할 때 역시도, **긍정 질문에 대한 대답과 늘 같아요!**
한국말처럼 긍정 질문과 부정 질문에 대한 대답이 다르지 않아요!
영어에서는, "Yes, I don't." 같은 불일치는 일어나지 않아요.

| Do you like it?<br>-Yes, I do. (응, 좋아해)<br>-No, I don't. (아니, 안 좋아해) | Don't you like it?<br>-Yes, I do. (응, 좋아해)<br>-No, I don't. (아니, 안 좋아해) |
|---|---|

<심화 표현>
"be supposed to" 하기로 되어 있다, 해야 돼.
Aren't you supposed to? (Shouldn't you?) 해야 되는 거 아니야?

| Aren't you supposed to be at school?<br>학교에 있어야 되는 거 아니야? | Don't you have to go to school?<br>학교 가야 되는 거 아니야? |
|---|---|

☞ 오른쪽 힌트를 이용해서, 직접 문장을 만들어보세요!

정답확인 : P 254

| 01 | 이게 저것보다 더 크지 않아?<br>-아니, 아닌 것 같아. (그렇게 생각하지 않아) 더 작아. | |
|---|---|---|
| 02 | 우리 지금 가야 되는 거 아니야?<br>-어, 가야 돼. 너 준비 다 됐어? | |
| 03 | 뭐라고 안 할 거야?<br>-아니, 난 아무 말도 안 할 거야. | |
| 04 | 가기 싫어?<br>-어, 가고 싶어. 근데 내가 시간이 있는지 모르겠어. | |
| 05 | 우리 지금 가면 안 돼?<br>-안돼. Jim을 기다려야 돼. | |
| 06 | 이거 네 것 아니야?<br>-어, 내 거야. 고마워. 이거 찾고 있었는데. | |
| 07 | 너 그거 아직 안 했어?<br>-아직 안 했어. | |
| 08 | 너 그거 없어?<br>-없어. 네 거 빌려도 돼? | |
| 09 | 너 뭐라고 말하지 않았어?<br>-아니, 아무 말도 안 했는데. | |
| 10 | 별로였어? (그거 안 좋았어?)<br>-좋았어. 나 좋은 시간 보냈어. | |

**Speaking Practice** 1min

☞ 오른쪽 힌트를 이용해서, 직접 문장을 만들어보세요!

| | | |
|---|---|---|
| 11 | 이거 별로야? (너 이거 안 좋아해?)<br>-좋아해. 선물 고마워.<br>🔊 | |
| 12 | 무슨 소리 못 들었어? (뭔가 안 들렸어?)<br>-아니. 뭘 들었어?<br>🔊 | |
| 13 | 오늘 날씨 좋지 않니?<br>-좋아.<br>🔊 | [날씨 좋은(날)<br>a beautiful day] |
| 14 | 우리 전에 만난 적 없었나?<br>-만난 적 있어.<br>🔊 | |
| 15 | 사고 아니었어?<br>-어, 사고였어.<br>🔊 | |
| 16 | 그거 비슷해야 되는 거 아니야?<br>-아니, 꼭 그렇지는 않아.<br>🔊 | [꼭 그렇지는 않아<br>Not really.] |
| 17 | 이것들 똑같아 보여. 같지 않니?<br>-아니. 모두 달라.<br>🔊 | |
| 18 | 내가 이거 내지 않았나?<br>-어, 냈어.<br>🔊 | [(돈) 내다 pay for] |
| 19 | 내가 너한테 말 안 했나?<br>-안 했어. 그래서, 그러고는 어떻게 됐어? (다음엔 무슨 일이 생겼어?)<br>🔊 | |
| 20 | 안 피곤해?<br>-아니, 난 괜찮아. 신경 써줘서 고마워.<br>🔊 | [고마워 Thank you for<br>신경 쓰다 care] |

Unit 4

☞ 오른쪽 힌트를 이용해서, 직접 문장을 만들어보세요!

| | | |
|---|---|---|
| 21 | 내가 뭐라도 가져와야 되는 거 아니야?<br>-아니. 그냥 몸만 와. (너 자신만 가져와) | [몸만 오다<br>bring oneself] |
| 22 | 그렇게 하는데 돈 많이 들지 않니?<br>-아니야. | |
| 23 | 고치는데 비싸지 않았어?<br>-어. 돈 많이 들었어. | |
| 24 | 거기 가는 데 오래 걸리지 않았어?<br>-어. 2시간 걸렸어. | |
| 25 | 너 이거 찾고 있지 않았어?<br>-어, 맞아. (네가 맞아) 이거 어디서 찾았어? | |
| 26 | 너 거기 자주 가지 않니?<br>-아니. 예전엔 그랬는데, 거기 안 가본 지 오래됐어. | |
| 27 | 너 예전에 그거 있지 않았어?<br>-어, 그랬어. | |
| 28 | 가끔은 그거 하는 거 어렵지 않니?<br>-어, 어려워. | |
| 29 | 너 이거 하려던 거 아니었어?<br>-어. 하지만 난 시간이 없었어. | |
| 30 | 그 애 이거 못 먹어?<br>-못 먹어. 견과류 알러지가 있어. | [알러지가 있는 allergic to<br>견과류 nuts] |

☞ 오른쪽 힌트를 이용해서, 직접 문장을 만들어보세요!

| | | |
|---|---|---|
| 31 | 너 지금 바쁜 거 아니야?<br>-바빠. 하지만 난 항상 널 위한 시간은 있어.<br>🔊 | |
| 32 | 너 거기 안 가봤어?<br>-안 가봤어. 언젠가는 가보고 싶어.<br>🔊 | [언젠가 someday] |
| 33 | 재미있지 않았니?<br>-어. 정말 재미있었어.<br>🔊 | [정말 재미있는<br>so much fun] |
| 34 | 그 애 달라 보이지 않니?<br>-어. 다른 사람 같아.<br>🔊 | |
| 35 | 그 애 목소리 속상해 보이지 않았어?<br>-아니. 괜찮아 보였어.<br>🔊 | [(목소리) ~처럼 보이다/들리다<br>sound] |
| 36 | 기다리는 게 낫지 않아?<br>-그래. 우리 확실히 알 때까지 기다리는 게 좋겠어.<br>🔊 | [확실히 알다<br>know for sure] |
| 37 | 배 안 고팠어?<br>-어. 배 엄청 고팠어.<br>🔊 | [엄청 배고픈 starving] |
| 38 | 조금 더 조심할 수 없어?<br>-미안. 더 조심할게.<br>🔊 | |
| 39 | 우리 이거 (에 대해) 뭔가 해야 되는 거 아니야?<br>(하는 게 좋지 않아?)<br>-어, 하지만 우리가 뭘 하는 게 좋은지 모르겠어.<br>🔊 | |
| 40 | 그 애 사랑스럽지 않니?<br>-어. 정말 귀여워.<br>🔊 | [사랑스러운 adorable] |

☞ 오른쪽 힌트를 이용해서, 직접 문장을 만들어보세요!

| 41 | 그 애는 이거 안 좋아해?<br>-좋아해. | |
| --- | --- | --- |
| 42 | 너 거기 안 갈 거야?<br>-안 갈 거야. 이번엔 싫어. | |
| 43 | 그거 거기 없었어?<br>-없었어. 다 봤는데, 못 찾았어. | [(찾으려고) 보다 look<br>다, 모든 곳 everywhere] |
| 44 | 내 말이 맞지 않니? (나랑 동의하지 않니?) 그렇지 않니?<br>(그렇게 생각지 않아?)<br>-그렇게 생각해. | [동의하다 agree with] |
| 45 | 오늘은 안 돼요? (너 이거 오늘 못해?)<br>-미안해, 오늘은 못 해요. | |
| 46 | 너 서둘러야 되는 거 아니야?<br>-서둘러야 돼. 시간 가는 줄 몰랐네. 알려줘서 고마워. | [시간 가는 줄 모르다<br>lose track of time<br>알려주다, 상기시키다 remind] |
| 47 | 그거 (돈) 더 들었어? 40불 아니었어?<br>-아니. 돈 더 들었어. | |
| 48 | 나랑 같이 가기 싫어?<br>-가고 싶어. | |
| 49 | 정말 좋지 않니?<br>-좋아. | |
| 50 | 너 뭔가 말하려던 거 아니었어?<br>-아니었어. | |

**Speaking Practice 1min**

☞ 오른쪽 힌트를 이용해서, 직접 문장을 만들어보세요!

| 51 | 몰랐어?<br>-몰랐어. | |
| --- | --- | --- |
| 52 | 시간 충분히 있지 않니?<br>-충분히 있어. | |
| 53 | 너 이거 안 할 거야?<br>-할 거야. 집에 가면 할 거야. | |
| 54 | 힘들지 않았니?<br>-힘들지 않았어. 그렇게 나쁘지 않았어. | [그렇게 나쁜 too bad] |
| 55 | 오래되지 않았니?<br>-어, 정말 오래됐어. | |
| 56 | 우리 지금 집에 가야 되는 거 아니야? (집에 가는 게 좋지 않을까?)<br>-그러는 게 좋겠어. | |
| 57 | 넌 안 가? (너 지금 안 와?)<br>-어, 가. (가고 있어) | |
| 58 | 너 지금 회사에 있어야 되는 거 아니야?<br>-아니, 오늘 쉬는 날이야. 내가 어제 너한테 말했잖아. | [~해야 돼, 하기로 되어있다 be supposed to] |
| 59 | 필기해야 되는 거 아니야?<br>(너 지금 필기하고 있어야 되는 거 아니야?) | [필기하다 take notes] |
| 60 | 우리가 그 애를 도와주어야 되는 거 아닌가?<br>(지금 도와주고 있어야) | |

Unit 4

## Speaking Practice
⏱ 1min

☞ 오른쪽 힌트를 이용해서, 직접 문장을 만들어보세요!

| | | |
|---|---|---|
| 61 | 그 애는 왜 이해를 못 하는 걸까? 🔊 | |
| 62 | 너 왜 안 왔어?<br>-미안, 막판에 일이 생겨서. (막판에 뭔가 생겼어) 🔊 | [생기다, 발생하다 come up<br>막판에 at the last minute ] |
| 63 | 너 왜 날 이해하지 않니?<br>슬프다. (그건 날 슬프게 만들어) 🔊 | |
| 64 | 그 애는 왜 안 오지?<br>-바쁜 것 같아. 🔊 | |
| 65 | 왜 나한테 이야기하지 않았어? (대화)<br>내가 아무것도 아니야? (내가 중요하지 않아?) 🔊 | [중요하다 matter] |
| 66 | 이거 왜 안 되지?<br>-몰라. 그거 그런지 며칠 됐어. 🔊 | |
| 67 | 너 그거 왜 안 했어?<br>하기 싫었니? 🔊 | |
| 68 | 너 왜 아무 말도 안 했어?<br>-그냥 할 수가 없었어. 🔊 | |
| 69 | 왜 나한테 말 안 했어?<br>-미안, 그러려고 했는데, 깜박했어. 🔊 | |
| 70 | 그게 왜 여기 없지?<br>봤니? 🔊 | |

# Speaking Practice — 1min

☞ 오른쪽 힌트를 이용해서, 직접 문장을 만들어보세요!

| 71 | 그 애는 왜 널 못 믿는 거야? | [믿다 trust] |
|---|---|---|
| 72 | 그는 왜 회사에 안 갔지? | |
| 73 | 너 지금 왜 일 안 해?<br>일하고 있어야 되는 거 아니야? | [해야 돼, 하기로 되어있다<br>be supposed to] |
| 74 | 너 이거 왜 안 좋아해? | |
| 75 | 왜 가기 싫은 건데? | |
| 76 | 이걸 내가 왜 모르고 있었지?<br>왜 진작 말하지 않았어? | [알고/인식하고 있는 aware of<br>진작, 더 빨리 sooner] |
| 77 | 왜 아무도 말 안 했지?<br>(왜 내게 이거에 대해 아무도 말하지 않았지?) | |
| 78 | 너 왜 안 놀랐어?<br>그럴 줄 알았니? (그런 일이 생길 줄 알았니?) | |
| 79 | 거기 안 가본 사람이 누가 있어? (누가 거기 안 가봤겠어?)<br>너무 유명해. 모두 거기 가봤어. | |
| 80 | 가끔씩 가지는 혼자만의 시간을 좋아하지 않는 사람이<br>누가 있어? (누가 때때로 평화와 조용함을 좋아하지 않겠어?) | [평화와 조용함 peace and quiet<br>때때로, 가끔씩 once in a while] |

# Speaking Practice
## 1min

### Do you not?
☞ 오른쪽 힌트를 이용해서, 직접 문장을 만들어보세요!

| | | |
|---|---|---|
| 81 | 너 정말 기억이 안 나?<br>-안 나. | |
| 82 | 너 정말 날 못 믿어?<br>-믿어. | |
| 83 | 너 진짜 내 말 못 들었어? (안 들렸어?)<br>-안 들렸어. 미안. | |
| 84 | 이거 정말 충분하지 않아?<br>-충분해. | |
| 85 | 나로는 안되겠어?<br>(내가 너한테 부족해?/충분히 좋지 않아?) | [충분한, 만족스러운<br>good enough (for)] |
| 86 | 내가 그에게 어울리지 않았나?<br>(충분하지 않았나?) | |
| 87 | 너 정말 그 책 안 읽어봤어? | |
| 88 | 너 정말 여기 있기 싫어? | |
| 89 | 너 이거 진짜 못 먹어? | |
| 90 | 그 말 하지 말아 줄래? | |

## Speaking Practice 1min

### Why don't I/you/we?
☞ 오른쪽 힌트를 이용해서, 직접 문장을 만들어보세요!

| 91 | 좀 앉는 게 어때? | [앉다 sit down] |
|---|---|---|
| 92 | 내가 가서 물 좀 가져다주는 게 어떻겠어? (널 위해서) | |
| 93 | 우리 잠깐 쉬는 게 어때? | [잠깐 쉬다 take five] |
| 94 | 생각해 볼 시간을 가지고, 네가 준비되면 알려주는 게 어때? 난 기다릴 수 있어. | |
| 95 | 내가 그거 어떻게 하는 건지 보여주는 게 어때? | |
| 96 | 우리 내일 오후에 미팅하는 게 어떻겠어? | |
| 97 | 한번 해보지 그래. 잃을 게 아무것도 없어. | [한번 해보다 give it a try] |
| 98 | 우리 아무 일 없는 척하는 게 어때? (아무 일도 일어나지 않은척하는 게 어때?) 그냥 평소처럼 해. | [가장하다/인척하다 pretend 평소처럼 하다 act normal] |
| 99 | 우리 거래하는 게 어때? 내가 이걸 널 위해서 하면, 너 날 위해 보답으로 뭔가 하는 거야. | [거래하다 make a deal 보답으로, 대신에 in return] |
| 100 | 내가 처리할게. (넌 그거에 대해서는 내게 맡기는 게 어때?) 걱정할 필요 없어. | [(~에게)맡기다, (~가)처리하다 let-worry 필요 없다 There's no need] |

Unit 4

# Review

복습 강의 바로 듣기

| Positive (긍정) | Negative (부정) | Question |
|---|---|---|
| So do I. | Neither do I. | - |
| 나도 | | - |
| Do you? | Don't you? | - |
| 그래? 정말? | | - |
| - | - | Who 동사? What 동사? |
| - | - | 누가? 뭐가? |
| - | - | Don't you? |
| - | - | 안 해? |

## stay & stay in touch

배운 내용을 생각하며, 직접 문장을 만들어보세요!

정답확인 : P 259

| 01 | 넌 여기 있는 게 좋을 것 같아. |
|---|---|
| 02 | 네가 안 가면, 나도 안 갈게. (네가 있으면, 나도 있을게) |
| 03 | 그 애는 더 오래 있을지도 몰라. [더 오래 longer] |
| 04 | 그 앤 한국에 오면 우리랑 같이 지내. |
| 05 | 너 저녁 먹고 가야 돼. [저녁 먹고 가다 stay for dinner] |
| 06 | 너 여기 있어도 돼.<br>-그래도 돼? |
| 07 | 그 애는 우리랑 잠시 동안 있을 거야. |
| 08 | 그건 오랫동안 기억에 남았어. (나와 함께 있었어) 내 머릿속에서 떠나질 않더라고. (내 머리 밖으로 못 내보냈어) [지워버리다, 생각 그만하다, 잊다 get sth out of one's head] |
| 09 | 거기 있으려고 했었는데, 마음을 바꿨어. |
| 10 | 월요일부터 여기서 지냈어. |
| 11 | 나는 일본에 갈 때마다 친구 집에서 지냈어.<br>(난 예전에 친구 집에 있었어, 내가 일본에 있을 때마다) [~때마다, 언제든지 whenever] |
| 12 | 그 애가 여기 얼마나 있을지 알고 싶어. |
| 13 | 나 여기 있고 싶어.<br>-나도. |
| 14 | (너) 여기 있지 그래. (여기 있지 뭐) |
| 15 | 나 여기 못 있겠어.<br>-나도. |

# Review

| | |
|---|---|
| 16 | 너 거기 있던 거 아니지? (거기 머무르고 있던 거 아니지, 그렇지?) |
| 17 | 거기서 더(이상) 오래 있을 수가 없었어. [더(이상) 오래 any longer] |
| 18 | 모든 게 바뀌어. (변화해) 아무것도 변하지 않는 것은 없어.<br>(아무것도 똑같이 머무르지 않아) |
| 19 | 나 아직 있을 곳을 못 찾았어. (있을 장소를 아직 찾지 않았어) |
| 20 | 나 며칠 여기 있어도 될까? |
| 21 | 난 거기에 있고 싶지 않았어.<br>-그랬어? |
| 22 | 우리 여기에 머무르지 않는 게 좋을 것 같아. |
| 23 | 너무 오래 민폐 끼치고 싶지 않아요.<br>[너무 오래 머무르다/민폐 끼치다 overstay one's welcome] |
| 24 | 나라면 너무 오래 머무르지 않을 거야. |
| 25 | 그 앤 여기 안 있을지도 몰라. 다른 곳을 찾을 수도 있어. [다른 곳 somewhere else] |
| 26 | 너 지금 친구들이랑 있는 거 아니지? |
| 27 | 네가 싫으면 우리 여기 안 있어도 돼. |
| 28 | 너 어디 머무르고 싶어? |
| 29 | 너 어디 있을 거야? 거기 얼마나 오래 있을 거야? |
| 30 | 어디서 있었어? |

## stay & stay in touch

배운 내용을 생각하며, 직접 문장을 만들어보세요!

| 31 | 우리 여기 있어야 돼? |
|---|---|
| 32 | 넌 어디에서 머무를 거 같아? |
| 33 | 우리 여기 있어도 돼? |
| 34 | 넌 어디에 있으려고 했어? |
| 35 | 그 애가 어디에서 머무르고 있는지 아니? |
| 36 | 여기서 머무른 지 얼마나 됐어요? |
| 37 | 호텔에 있지 않았어? |
| 38 | 여기 있기 싫어? |
| 39 | 누가 여기 있었어? |
| 40 | 그 앤 중국 가면 어디서 머물러? |
| 41 | 너 머무를 수 있는 곳(어딘가) 있어? |
| 42 | **연락해, 알았지?** [연락하다 (계속) stay in touch] |
| 43 | 우린 몇 년 동안은 연락을 했었어. 그리고 연락이 끊어졌어.<br>[연락 끊어지다 lose contact] |
| 44 | 너랑 계속 연락하고 싶어. |
| 45 | 우린 2008년에 내가 일본 갔을 때 만났어. 그때 이후로 계속 연락하고 있어.<br>[그때 이후로 (계속/쭉) ever since] |

Unit 4

# Dialogue Practice

**Making suggestions**

**A**: Why don't we try something different?

**B**: Okay, what do you have in mind?


**A**: Let's do something fun!

**B**: I'm in! / Count me in!


**A**: Shall we start now?

**B**: That's a good idea!


**A**: We could go to the movies.

**B**: Yes, that sounds good.


**A**: It's raining outside. We might as well stay in.

**B**: Okay. Let's do that.

**A**: How about meeting at 7 tomorrow? (How about we meet at 7 tomorrow?)

**B**: Sorry, I can't. I have other plans.

**A**: What about doing the presentation together? (What about we do the presentation together?)

**B**: I'd rather not. I work better alone.

## Dialogue Practice

**Making suggestions**

**A**: 우리 (뭔가) 다른 걸 해보는 게 어때? [다른 것 something different]

**B**: 오케이, 생각해 둔 게 있어? (뭐가 네 마음에 있어?) [생각해두다 have in mind]

**A**: (뭔가) 재미난 거 하자! [재미난 거 something fun]

**B**: 난 할래! (난 in 이야!) / 나도 끼워줘! (나도 넣어줘) [나도 할래 I'm in! 나도 끼워줘! Count me in, (too)!]

**A**: 우리 지금 시작할까?

**B**: 좋은 생각이야!

**A**: 우리 영화 보러 가도 되고. [~해도 되고 we could]

**B**: 응, 좋아. (그 소리 좋다)

**A**: 밖에 비 와. 우리 그냥 안에 있지 뭐. [안에 있다 stay in]

**B**: 그래. 그렇게 하자.

A: 내일 7시에 만나는 거 어때?

B: 미안, 난 못 해. 다른 약속 (계획) 이 있어. [다른 약속 other plans]

A: 우리 프리젠테이션 같이 하는 게 어때?

B: 안 그러는 게 낫겠어. 난 혼자 (일) 더 잘해. [안 하고 싶어, 안 하는 게 좋겠어 I'd rather not 더 잘하다 work better]

### Making suggestions

Why don't we? [하는 게 어때?]
Let's [하자]
Shall we? [할까?]
We could [우리 ~해도 되고]
We might as well [하지 뭐]
How about -ing? [~하는 게 어때?]
What about -ing? [~하는 게 어때?]

# Unit

# 5

과거 이전의 일을
말하고 싶을 때

## Unit 5

### 과거 이전의 일을 말하고 싶을 때

# had p.p. "했었어"

"had p.p." 는 과거완료라고 하기도 하고, '대과거'라고 하기도 해요. 과거의 이야기를 할 때에는 처음부터 끝까지 일어난 순서대로 나열하기가 힘들어요. 이럴 때, had p.p. 를 사용하면, 과거 이전에 일어난 이야기를 표현할 수 있어요. 또한, had p.p. 는 현재완료의 과거 형태이므로, 현재완료와 동일하게 과거 이전의 어느 시점부터 그 과거까지의 시간을 포함해서 이야기할 수도 있어요.

|  | Positive (긍정) | Negative (부정) | Question (의문) |
|---|---|---|---|
| 과거완료 | I had p.p. | I hadn't p.p. | Had you p.p.? |
|  | 했어, 했었어 (그전에) | 안 했어, 안 했었어 | 했어? 했었어? |
| 과거완료진행 | I had been -ing | I hadn't been -ing | Had you been -ing? |
|  | 했었어 (계속)<br>하고 있었어 | 안 했었어<br>안 하고 있었어 | 했었어?<br>하고 있었어? |

> 이렇게 만듭니다!

had 뒤에 p.p. 를 넣어주면 돼요!

| 긍정 | 부정 | 의문 |
|---|---|---|
| I had done it before.<br>나 그거 전에 해봤었어. | I hadn't done it before.<br>나 그거 전에 안 해봤었어. | Had you done it before?<br>그거 전에 해봤었어? |
| I had been waiting for 2 hours.<br>(그전에) 두 시간 기다렸었어. | I hadn't been waiting long.<br>오래 기다리지 않았었어. | Had you been waiting long?<br>오래 기다렸었어? |

<주의>

had p.p. 는 과거 이전의 일을 이야기하는 것이라 과거형이랑 주로 사용해요.
어떤 일이 순서대로 일어난 것을 나열한다면 굳이 사용하지 않아요!

<비교>

| 과거 | He came and we had dinner together. |
|---|---|
| 과거진행 | He came when we were having dinner. |
| 과거완료 | We had had dinner when he came. |

| 현재완료 have p.p. | 과거완료 had p.p. |
|---|---|
| I want to watch this movie.<br>I haven't seen it yet. | I wanted to watch that movie.<br>I hadn't seen it before. |

## 긍정문

☞ 오른쪽 힌트를 이용해서, 직접 문장을 만들어보세요!

정답확인 : P 260

| 01 | 우리가 거기 갔을 때, 영화는 이미 시작했어. | |
|---|---|---|
| 02 | 내가 도착했을 때, (그들) 벌써 문을 닫았더라고.<br>그래서, 아무것도 못 샀어. | |
| 03 | 내가 집에 왔을 때, 모두 자더라고. | [자다 go to bed] |
| 04 | Jim이 거기 도착했을 때, Sue는 벌써 갔어. (떠났어) | |
| 05 | 내가 일어났을 때, 그는 벌써 회사 갔어. | [~로 가다, 나가다<br>leave for] |
| 06 | 우리 영화 같이 봤어.<br>근데, 난 전에 그거 봤었어. | |
| 07 | 나 인천에 갔었어.<br>우리는 강원도 가고 싶었었는데, 안 그러기로 했어. | [하기로 하다<br>decide (not) to] |
| 08 | 나 이거 내 생일 선물로 받았어.<br>이거 늘 갖고 싶어 했었던 거야. | [(~로) 받다 get for] |
| 09 | 그거 잃어버렸을 때, 정말 속상했어.<br>오랫동안 가지고 있었는데.<br>그건 내게 소중한 추억이 있는 거였는데. | [추억 있는 소중한<br>(have) sentimental value for] |
| 10 | 나 작년에 내 예전 차 팔았어.<br>거의 10년 몰았었지. | [예전차 old car<br>거의 nearly] |

# Speaking Practice 1min

## 긍정문

☞ 오른쪽 힌트를 이용해서, 직접 문장을 만들어보세요!

| | | |
|---|---|---|
| 11 | 저번 주말은 편안했어.<br>계속 너무 바빴고, 난 그게 필요했었어.<br>🔊 | [편안한, 쉬는 relaxing] |
| 12 | 그거 완전 재미났어. 나 진짜 재미있었어.<br>재미가 뭔지 잊고 있었어.<br>🔊 | [완전 재미난 a blast<br>재미있다, 잘 놀다<br>have (so much) fun] |
| 13 | 나 그거 이미 알고 있었어.<br>누군가 내게 말해줬어.<br>🔊 | |
| 14 | 알아. (나 그거 알고 있었어)<br>네가 벌써 그거 말했잖아.<br>🔊 | |
| 15 | 나 알고 있었어.<br>네가 경고해 줬잖아. 기억 안 나?<br>🔊 | [알다, 인지하다 be aware of<br>위험하다고 말하다(경고)<br>warn] |
| 16 | 난 가고 싶지 않았어, 거기 많이 가봤어서.<br>🔊 | |
| 17 | 난 미리 티켓들을 예약했었어.<br>-나도. 티켓 구하기 힘들 줄 알았어.<br>🔊 | [미리 in advance] |
| 18 | 난 Jim이 하기 전에 했어.<br>🔊 | |
| 19 | 난 모두 오기 전에 도착했어.<br>내가 1등으로 도착했어. (내가 도착한 첫 사람이었어)<br>🔊 | [1등, 첫 사람<br>the first one (to)] |
| 20 | 나 그 애랑 이야기 못 했어.<br>이야기할 수 있기 전에 그 애가 갔어. (떠났어)<br>🔊 | |

## 긍정문

☞ 오른쪽 힌트를 이용해서, 직접 문장을 만들어보세요!

| 21 | 처음 해본 거 아니야. (내 처음 아니었어) 전에 했었어.<br>-나도. | [처음 해보는, 처음인 one's first time] |
|---|---|---|
| 22 | 그는 지난 달에 회사를 그만뒀어. (떠났어)<br>거기서 15년 일했는데. | [회사 the firm] |
| 23 | 그를 떠나기 쉽지 않았어.<br>우리 사귄 지 5년 되었었어. | [사귀는 together] |
| 24 | 나 그 영화 다시 봤어.<br>전에 봤긴 했는데. 또 보고 싶었어. | |
| 25 | 나 그거 못 찾았어.<br>비록 다 찾아봤음에도 불구하고. | [비록, ~에도 불구하고 even though<br>(찾아)보다 look ] |
| 26 | 나 미팅에 늦었었어, 기차를 놓쳤었거든. | [늦은 late for] |
| 27 | 난 그 애한테 말 안 해도 됐어.<br>그 애 이미 알고 있었어. | |
| 28 | 우린 좋은 친구였어.<br>우리 한 5살 때부터인가 서로 알았었어. | [한, 아마 maybe] |
| 29 | 그건 정말 엉망이었어.<br>그가 정말 큰 피해를 끼쳤어. | [엉망, 난장판 (such) a mess<br>피해/손해 끼치다<br>do (so much) damage] |
| 30 | 그 애는 주체할 수 없을 정도로 울고 있었어.<br>무슨 일이 있었던 거지. (뭔가 그에게 일어났었어) | [주체할 수 없이 울다 cry uncontrollably] |

## Speaking Practice (1min)

### 긍정문

☞ 오른쪽 힌트를 이용해서, 직접 문장을 만들어보세요!

| | | |
|---|---|---|
| 31 | 난 그에게 뭔가 나쁜 일이 생겼다는 걸 알았어. | [뭔가 나쁜 something bad] |
| 32 | 그는 영웅이었어.<br>생전에 훌륭한 일들을 했어. | [훌륭한 일들 great things<br>생전에 in life] |
| 33 | 그는 내게 정말 많이 가르쳐 줬었어.<br>난 그가 여전히 그리워. | [정말 많이 so much] |
| 34 | 난 그에게 정말 많이 배웠었어.<br>그는 내가 본받고 싶은 사람이었어. | [본받고 싶은 사람, 롤모델 role model] |
| 35 | 넌 내가 뭘 원했는지 알고 있었지, 그렇지? | |
| 36 | 난 그가 무엇을 필요로 했는지 알고 있었어,<br>하지만 그걸 그에게 주지는 못했어. | |
| 37 | 내가 무슨 짓을 했는지 너무 늦게 알았지.<br>(내가 뭘 한 건지 깨닫지 않았어, 그게 너무 늦기 전까지는) | [알다, 깨닫다 realize ] |
| 38 | 난 그가 내게 어떤 의미였었는지 미처 몰랐어.<br>(그가 내게 무슨 의미였었는지 깨닫지 않았어) | [의미 있다, 중요하다 mean to sb] |
| 39 | 난 그 애가 어디 갔는지 몰랐어.<br>그는 내게 아무 말도 안 했었어. | |
| 40 | 내가 옳은 일을 한 건지 (아닌지) 모르겠더라고. | [옳은 일을 하다 do the right thing] |

Unit 5

# Speaking Practice 1min

## 긍정문

☞ 오른쪽 힌트를 이용해서, 직접 문장을 만들어보세요!

| | | |
|---|---|---|
| 41 | 뭔가 빼먹은 거 같더라니.<br>(난 뭔가 까먹은듯한 느낌이었어) | [~한 느낌이다 feel like] |
| 42 | 나 집에 다시 가야 됐어.<br>서류 가져오는 걸 깜빡했었거든. | [서류 the documents] |
| 43 | 난 아무것도 먹지 않았어,<br>왜냐면 점심을 많이 먹었었거든. | [점심 많이 먹다<br>eat a big lunch] |
| 44 | 속이 안 좋았어.<br>아이스크림을 너무 많이 먹었었거든. | [속이 안 좋다, 아프다 feel sick<br>너무 많이 too much] |
| 45 | 그런 말 전에 많이 들어봤었었지. | [정말 많이 so many times] |
| 46 | 나 그 영화 보기 전에 책 읽었었어. | |
| 47 | 그 애는 속상해했어.<br>반지를 잃어버렸었거든. | |
| 48 | 더 이상 할 게 없었어. (할게 아무것도 남지 않았었어)<br>내가 할 수 있었던 모든 것을 했어. | |
| 49 | 내가 무슨 일을 겪었는지 아무도 몰랐어.<br>아무에게도 말하지 않았었어. | [힘든 상황인, 겪는<br>(go) through] |
| 50 | 네가 무슨 말을 했었는지 생각이 안 났어.<br>(기억을 못 했어) | |

## Speaking Practice 1min

### 부정문

☞ 오른쪽 힌트를 이용해서, 직접 문장을 만들어보세요!

| | | |
|---|---|---|
| 51 | 그 애를 봐서 정말 좋았어.<br>우리 서로 안 본 지 오래되었었거든. | |
| 52 | Wendy가 누군지 난 몰랐어.<br>난 전에 그 애를 만나본 적 없었어. | |
| 53 | 내가 그거 찾으러 거기 갔을 때, 그들은 내 차를 고쳐놓지 않았어. 오늘 거기 다시 가야 돼. | |
| 54 | 나 너무 배고팠어.<br>아침 이후로 아무것도 안 먹었었어. | |
| 55 | 정말 좋았어. 전에 거기 가본적 없었어.<br>처음 가봤어. (내 처음이었어) | [처음 가/해 본<br>one's first time] |
| 56 | 난 놀랐었어.<br>아무것도 기대하지 않았었는데. | |
| 57 | 난 그를 믿었었어.<br>전에 내게 거짓말한 적 없었는데. | |
| 58 | 난 그거 기대 안 하고 있었는데.<br>이럴 줄 몰랐어. | [예상하다, ~할 줄/이럴 줄 알다<br>see it coming] |
| 59 | 정말 억울했어! 그건 내 잘못이 아니었어.<br>난 아무것도 잘못한 게 없어. | [억울한, 불공평한 unfair] |
| 60 | 그거 처음 해봤어. (그거 내 첫 시도였어)<br>전에 그거 해본 적 없어. | [처음 해보는 one's first try] |

## Speaking Practice 1min

### 부정문

☞ 오른쪽 힌트를 이용해서, 직접 문장을 만들어보세요!

| | | |
|---|---|---|
| 61 | 나 전에 거기 한 번도 가본 적이 없었어.<br>전에 가보지 않은 곳(어딘가)을 가고 싶었거든. | [한 번도 never] |
| 62 | 정말 아름다웠어.<br>전에 그런 걸 한 번도 본 적이 없었어. | [그런 것<br>anything like that] |
| 63 | 대단했어!<br>전에 그런 걸 경험해 본 적이 없었어. | [대단한 incredible] |
| 64 | 새로운 경험이었어.<br>그런 걸 전에 한 적이 없었어. | |
| 65 | 모든 게 똑같았어.<br>아무것도 바뀌지 않았었어. | |
| 66 | 그는 똑같아 보였어.<br>조금도 변하지 않았어. | [조금도 a bit] |
| 67 | 모든 게 그냥 괜찮았어.<br>아무 일도 일어나지 않았었어. | [괜찮은 fine] |
| 68 | 왜 아무 일도 일어나지 않았던 척했어? | [~인척하다, 가장하다<br>pretend] |
| 69 | 문제가 있었던 것 같아.<br>우리 거기 머무른 지 한 시간이나 되었었고,<br>쇼는 시작도 안 했었어. | [~(조차)도 even] |
| 70 | 오랜만에 이야기해서 좋았어.<br>우리 서로 이야기 안 한 지 오래됐었거든. | [오랜만에 이야기하다<br>catch up] |

## Speaking Practice 1min

### 부정문

☞ 오른쪽 힌트를 이용해서, 직접 문장을 만들어보세요!

| | | |
|---|---|---|
| 71 | 난 그거에 대해서 몰랐어.<br>그는 내게 아무 말도 안 했었어. | |
| 72 | 난 몰랐었어.<br>아무도 (아무것도) 말하지 않았었어. | [알다, 인지하다 be aware of] |
| 73 | 처음 들어본 거였어. (그건 내가 들어본 처음이었어)<br>너 나한테 말 안 했었어. | |
| 74 | 네가 나한테 말해줄 때까지 몰랐었어. | [알다, 깨닫다 realize] |
| 75 | 가게에 내 폰을 두고 왔어.<br>집에 올 때까지 몰랐었어. | |
| 76 | 정말? 몰랐어. (알아차리지 않았었어) | [알다, 알아차리다, 보이다 notice] |
| 77 | 그게 바로 거기 있었는데, 난 보이지도 않았어. | [바로 right<br>~(조차)도 even] |
| 78 | 어떻게 그런 생각을 했어?<br>난 생각도 안 해봤어. | [생각하다, 새 아이디어 내다 come up with] |
| 79 | 난 그런 생각 해본 적도 없어.<br>(꿈도 안 꿔봤어) | [꿈꾸다 dream of] |
| 80 | 또 다른 상을 받을 거라고는 꿈도 꾸지 않았었어요. | [또 다른 상 another award] |

# Speaking Practice 1min

## 의문문

☞ 오른쪽 힌트를 이용해서, 직접 문장을 만들어보세요!

| | | |
|---|---|---|
| 81 | 여기 전에 와본 적 있었어, 아니면 처음이었어? | |
| 82 | 넌 그거 벌써 봤었니? | |
| 83 | 그 애가 떠나기 전에 내게 아무거라도 남겼었어? | |
| 84 | 너 그거 팔기 전에 얼마나 가지고 있었었어? | |
| 85 | 너 캐나다 가기 전에 영어 공부했었어? | |
| 86 | 너 여기 오기 전에 뭐 했어? | |
| 87 | 그날 어디 갔다 왔었어? | [그날 that day] |
| 88 | 내가 할 만큼 하지 않았었어? (충분히 하지 않았었어?)<br>더 이상은 그렇게 살 수 없었어. | [더 이상 any longer] |
| 89 | 너 그 영화 보기 전에 책 읽지 않았었어? | |
| 90 | 내가 오기 전에 무슨 일이 있었었어? | |

**Speaking Practice 1min**

**had been -ing**

☞ 오른쪽 힌트를 이용해서, 직접 문장을 만들어보세요!

| | | |
|---|---|---|
| 91 | 그거 드디어 어제 왔어.<br>몇 달을 기다렸었어. | [드디어 finally<br>몇 달을, 오래 for months] |
| 92 | 너 어디 있었어?<br>계속 전화했었는데. | |
| 93 | 안 그래도 너의 주말에 대해 묻고 싶었는데,<br>자꾸 까먹었어. | [안 그래도 ~하려고 하다<br>mean to<br>자꾸/계속하다 keep -ing] |
| 94 | 힘든 시간이었어.<br>우린 아기 가지려고 오랫동안 시도했었어. | [힘든 시간<br>a difficult time] |
| 95 | 그는 일 년째 바람을 피우고 있었어. | [바람피우다<br>cheat on sb] |
| 96 | 알고 보니, 수년 동안 그래왔더라고.<br>(그런 일이 일어나고 있었더라고) | [알고 보니, 보아하니 apparently<br>(일) 일어나다 go on] |
| 97 | 피곤했어.<br>하루 종일 일을 했었어. | |
| 98 | 나 그거 누구 줬어.<br>오랫동안 가지고 있었지만, 쓰지는 않았었어. | [누구 주다 give-away] |
| 99 | 난 너 오기 전에 막 도착했어.<br>오래 기다리지 않았어. | |
| 100 | 그날 오전에 넌 뭘 하고 있었어? | [그날 오전 that morning] |

# Review

복습 강의 바로 듣기

| Positive (긍정) | Negative (부정) | Question |
|---|---|---|
| So do I. | Neither do I. | - |
| 나도 || - |
| Do you? | Don't you? | - |
| 그래? 정말? || - |
| - | - | Who 동사? What 동사? |
| - | - | 누가? 뭐가? |
| - | - | Don't you? |
| - | - | 안 해? |
| I had p.p. | I hadn't p.p. | Had you p.p.? |
| 했어, 했었어 (그전에) | 안 했어, 안 했었어 | 했어? 했었어? |
| I had been -ing | I hadn't been -ing | Had you been -ing? |
| 했었어 (계속)<br>하고 있었어 | 안 했었어<br>안 하고 있었어 | 했었어?<br>하고 있었어? |

## hear & hear-out

배운 내용을 생각하며, 직접 문장을 만들어보세요!

정답확인 : P 263

| 01 | 네 말 잘 들려. (잘 들을 수 있어) 소리 그만 질러! [그만하다 stop -ing] |
|---|---|
| 02 | 어, 들었어. 넌 어때? |
| 03 | (나) 네 이야기 들어봐야 돼. (네 쪽 이야기 들어야 돼)<br>[~(쪽/편)의 이야기 one's side of the story] |
| 04 | 만나서 정말 반가워요. 이야기 많이 들었어요. (너에 대해 정말 많이 들었어요)<br>[정말 많이 so much] |
| 05 | 전부 다 듣고 싶어. (그거에 대한 모두 듣고 싶어) |
| 06 | 네 목소리를 들어서 정말 좋아. 네가 전화해서 난 기뻐. |
| 07 | 연락 기다릴게요. (곧 너로부터 소식 듣기를 기대합니다) [기대/고대하다 look forward to -ing] |
| 08 | 딱 기다려. (넌 나한테서 곧 듣게 될 거야) |
| 09 | 나 이건 처음 듣는 건데. (이게 처음이야, 내가 이것에 대해 듣고 있는) |
| 10 | 그거 전에 많이 들어봤지. [많이, 여러 번 many times]<br>-나도. |
| 11 | 나 예전엔 그 말 많이 들었었어. [많이 a lot]<br>-그랬어? |
| 12 | 연락해 줘서 고마웠어. (너로부터 소식 들어서 좋았어) |
| 13 | 넌 그거는 그 애한테 듣는 게 좋겠어. |
| 14 | 요즘 귀에서 이명 소리가 들려. [이명 소리 들리다 hear ringing in one's ears] |
| 15 | (나 그거) 알고 있었어. Kim 한테 들었었어. |

# Review

| | |
|---|---|
| 16 | 듣고 싶지 않아. |
| 17 | 네 말 안 들려. (네 말 못 듣겠어) 네 소리가 끊기는데. [소리/전화 끊기다 break up] |
| 18 | 난 아무 소리 안 들리는데. |
| 19 | 그런 거 들어본 적 없어. (한 번도 그거 들어본 적 없어) [~에 대해 듣다 hear of] |
| 20 | 알았어, 말해줄게. 하지만 내가 말했다고 하면 안 돼. (넌 나한테 듣지 않았어) |
| 21 | 참 나, 그 말이 아니야. (넌 내 말을 듣고 있지 않아) 그런 뜻이 아니야. (그건 내가 의미하는 게 아니야) [내가 의미하는 거 what I mean] |
| 22 | 5분 안에 나한테서 연락 없으면, 경찰에 전화해. (네가 나한테 소식 안 들으면) |
| 23 | 난 아무 소리도 못 들었어.<br>-그랬어? |
| 24 | 너무 시끄러웠어. 아무것도 못 들었어. |
| 25 | 우린 그 애한테 소식 못 들은 지 오래됐어. |
| 26 | (난 그 말) 안 들어도 돼. |
| 27 | 그의 청력이 좋지 않아. 보청기가 필요해. [청력 hearing 보청기 hearing aids] |
| 28 | 고등학교 때 이후로 처음 들어봤어. (고등학교 이후로 그 말 안 들었어)<br>-나도. |
| 29 | 아무도 우리의 소리를 듣지 못해. |
| 30 | 못 들었어. (안 들었어) 뭐라고 했니? |

## hear & hear-out

배운 내용을 생각하며, 직접 문장을 만들어보세요!

| | |
|---|---|
| 31 | 내가 (그 말) 들어야 돼? |
| 32 | 내 말 들려? (너 내말 들을 수 있어?) |
| 33 | 저 소리 들려? |
| 34 | 무슨 말 들었어? 그걸 어디서 들었어? |
| 35 | 나 좋은 소식이랑 나쁜 소식이 있는데. 어느 거 먼저 들을래? |
| 36 | (너 그 말) 들었어? 우리가 이겼어! |
| 37 | 그는 은퇴할 거래. (은퇴할 거야) [은퇴하다 retire] 너 이거 듣고 있어? |
| 38 | 내가 들어도 돼? |
| 39 | 네가 무슨 말을 들었는지 말해줄래? |
| 40 | 내 말 못 들었어? (안 들었어?) |
| 41 | 언제 연락할 거야? (내가 언제 너한테 소식 들을 수 있어?) |
| 42 | 내 말 좀 들어봐, 응? [hear sb out (말/이야기 잘/끝까지) 듣다] |
| 43 | 내 말 좀 들어줄래? |
| 44 | 난 우리가 그 애의 이야기를 들어주는 게 좋을 것 같아. |
| 45 | 그 애 이야기를 들어주는 게 어때? |

# Dialogue Practice

**My best trip ever!**

My best trip ever was to Egypt last year. I had wanted to go there for a long time. I had wanted to see the Pyramids, and ancient temples.

Before my trip to Egypt, I had been saving money for 3 years. When I finally booked the tickets, I was so excited. I had been waiting for that moment for a long time.

It was my first time traveling solo. I had never traveled alone before. I hadn't dared to travel alone, let alone to a foreign country. I had been very nervous. So, I booked an organized tour. I traveled with a group and a local tour guide. It made me feel safe, and it was a good choice. I had so much fun!

Before I picked a tour package, I had searched and learned everything about Egypt. This was very helpful, because I knew what I had wanted to see, and where I had wanted to visit.

When I saw the Egyptian Pyramids, I was in awe. I had never seen such beautiful sights before I went to Egypt. I had never experienced anything like that in my life!

# Dialogue Practice

**My best trip ever! (내 평생 최고의 여행!)**

내 평생 최고의 여행은 작년에 Egypt(로)였다.
거기에 오랫동안 가고 싶었었다.
Pyramids랑 고대 신전들을 보고 싶었었다. [고대 신전들 ancient temples]

나의 Egypt로의 여행 전에, 3년 동안 돈을 모았다. [돈 모으다 save money]
내가 마침내 티켓들을 예매했을 때는, 정말 기분이 좋았다.
(흥분했었다) [티켓 예매하다 book the tickets]
그 순간을 정말 오랫동안 기다려왔었다.

(그건) 내 첫 솔로 여행이었다. (그건 솔로 여행한 (내) 처음이었다)
[처음인 one's first time -ing 솔로 여행하다 travel solo]
전에 혼자 여행해 본 적이 한 번도 (절대) 없었다.
혼자 여행하는 것을 (감히) 도전해 본 적 없었다, 하물며 외국으로는 고사하고. [감히~(도전) 하다, 용기 내다 dare to 하물며/커녕, 고사하고 let alone 외국 a foreign country]
난 매우 불안했었다. 그래서, 패키지 투어를 예매했다.
[패키지 투어 an organized tour]
난 하나의 그룹, 그리고 지역 투어가이드와 함께 여행했다.
그건 내가 안전하다고 느끼게 해주었고, (내가 안전한 느낌으로 만들었다)
(그건) 좋은 선택이었다. (난) 정말 재미있었다!

내가 투어 패키지를 고르기 전에, 난 Egypt의 모든 것에 대해 검색하고 배웠다. [투어 패키지 a tour package 검색하다 search]
이건 매우 도움이 되었다, 내가 뭘 보고 싶은지, 어디를 방문하고 싶은지를 알았기 때문이다.

(내가) Egyptian Pyramids를 봤을 땐, 경탄을 금치 못했다.
[경탄을 금치 못하는, 감탄/경외하는 in awe]
Egypt에 가기 전에, 난 그런 아름다운 광경들을 한 번도 (절대) 본 적이 없었다. [그런 아름다운 광경들 such beautiful sights]
내 인생에서 그런 것은 한 번도 경험해 본 적이 없었다! [그런 것 anything like that]

# Unit

# 6

상대에게 바라는 걸
말하고 싶을 때

## Unit 6

### 상대에게 바라는 걸 말하고 싶을 때

# I want you to "하면 좋겠어"

대화에서 "want to"는 하고 싶은 것 혹은 하기 싫은 것을 표현할 수 있어서 정말 많이 사용되는데요. 그 가운데에 다른 사람이나 대상을 넣어서, 그 상대에게 바라는 것을 말할 때도 사용할 수 있어요!
특히 의문문의 경우, 상대가 내게 원하는 것을 직접 물어봄으로써 "할까?" 라는 표현으로 굉장히 자주 사용합니다.

| Positive | Negative | Question |
| --- | --- | --- |
| I want you to | I don't want you to | Do you want me to? |
| 하면 좋겠어<br>하길 바라 | 안 하면 좋겠어<br>안 하길 바라 | 할까? 하면 좋겠어?<br>하길 바라? |
| I expect you to | I don't expect you to | Do you expect me to? |
| 하길 바라 (기대해) | 안 하길 바라 (기대해) | 하길 바라? (기대해?) |
| I would like you to | I wouldn't like you to | Would you like me to? |
| 하면 좋겠어<br>하길 바라 | 안 하면 좋겠어<br>안 하길 바라 | 할까? 하면 좋겠어?<br>하길 바라? |
| I need you to | I don't need you to | Do you need me to? |
| 꼭 하면 좋겠어 | 할 필요 없어 | 해줄까? 하면 돼? |

"want" 를 사용해서 바라는 걸 표현하기도 하지만, 그것을 기대한다는 느낌으로 "expect" 를 사용하기도 해요. "want to" 와 동일한 표현인 "I'd like to" 도 사용할 수 있고요.
"need" 를 쓰면 좀 더 강하게 바라는 것을 말할 수 있어요.

> 이렇게 만듭니다!

"I want + 대상 + to 동사원형"

"want" 와 "to" 사이에 바라는 상대나 대상을 넣어주면 돼요!

| 긍정 | 부정 | 의문 |
| --- | --- | --- |
| I want this to end.<br>이게 끝나면 좋겠어. | I don't want this to end.<br>이게 안 끝나면 좋겠어. | Do you want this to end?<br>이게 끝나면 좋겠어? |
| I wanted you to know.<br>난 네가 알기를 바랐어. | I didn't want anyone to know.<br>난 아무도 모르길 바랐어. | Did you want him to know?<br>그가 알기를 바랐어? |

<비교>

| want me to | Do you want me to come? | 내가 올까? 내가 오면 좋겠어?<br>(넌 그걸 바라?) |
| --- | --- | --- |
| should | Should I come? | 내가 오는 게 좋을까?<br>(그게 맞는지, 좋은 건지) |
| shall | Shall I come? | 내가 올까?<br>(제안) |

# Speaking Practice 1min

## 긍정문

☞ 오른쪽 힌트를 이용해서, 직접 문장을 만들어보세요!

정답확인 : P 264

| 01 | 난 네가 가면 좋겠어.<br>지금 너랑 얘기 못하겠어. | |
|---|---|---|
| 02 | 난 Jenny가 파티에 오면 좋겠어.<br>그 애 초대할 수 있어? | |
| 03 | 네가 그 애한테서 떨어졌으면 좋겠어.<br>알겠어? (너 내말 들려?) | [떨어지다, 멀리하다<br>stay away from] |
| 04 | 넌 우리가 잘 지내길 바라지? | [잘 (친하게) 지내다<br>get along] |
| 05 | 네가 생각해 보면 좋겠어. | |
| 06 | 네 마음에 있는 게 뭐든 말하면 좋겠어.<br>나한텐 솔직해도 돼. | [뭐든 whatever<br>마음에 있는 on one's mind<br>솔직한 honest with] |
| 07 | 네가 그 애한테 말하면 좋겠어. | |
| 08 | 네가 진정하면 좋겠어. | [진정하다 calm down] |
| 09 | 난 그 애도 날 사랑하면 좋겠어.<br>그게 그렇게 잘못된 거야? | [~도 사랑하다 love-back<br>그렇게 so] |
| 10 | 난 그 애가 벌받으면 좋겠어.<br>고통받았으면 좋겠어. | [벌받다, 대가 치르다 pay<br>고통받다 suffer] |

기초영어 1000문장 말하기 연습 4

## Speaking Practice 1min

### 긍정문
☞ 오른쪽 힌트를 이용해서, 직접 문장을 만들어보세요!

| | | |
|---|---|---|
| 11 | 난 모두가 진실을 알길 바라. | |
| 12 | 내가 정말 다 미안하다는 거 네가 알면 좋겠어.<br>(모든 게 얼마나 미안한지 알길 바라) | [정말 미안하다<br>how sorry I am (for)] |
| 13 | 내가 얼마나 미안했는지 네가 알았으면 했어. | |
| 14 | 내가 그 앨 얼마나 사랑했는지 그가 알길 바랐어. | |
| 15 | 내가 널 위해 여기 있다는 걸 네가 알면 좋겠어. | |
| 16 | 그는 우리가 이걸 오늘까지 마무리하길 원해.<br>우리 낭비할 시간이 없어. | [마무리하다, 끝내다<br>finish] |
| 17 | 네가 옳은 일을 하길 바라. | |
| 18 | 네가 날 지지하길 바라. 네가 내 편이면 좋겠어.<br>그게 내가 원하는 전부야. (그게 내가 원하는 모두야) | [~편인 on one's side] |
| 19 | 네가 날 기다리면 좋겠어. | |
| 20 | 이거 네 거야. (널 위한 거야)<br>그 애는 네가 이걸 가지길 원했을 거야. | |

## Speaking Practice 1min

## 긍정문

☞ 오른쪽 힌트를 이용해서, 직접 문장을 만들어보세요!

| 21 | 그는 내가 그를 위해 모든 걸 하길 바래. (기대해) | [기대하다<br>expect sb to ] |
|---|---|---|
| 22 | 난 네가 더 잘하길 바라. (기대해) | |
| 23 | 네가 날 꼭 믿어줘야 돼.<br>(날 위해) 그래 줄 수 있어? | [(꼭) 해줘야 돼<br>need sb to ] |
| 24 | 네가 날 데리러 와줘야 돼.<br>나 여기서 나가고 싶어. | [데리러 오다<br>come (and) get me<br>나가다 get out of ] |
| 25 | 난 이게 정말(간절히) 되길 바라.<br>이게 잘되면 좋겠어. | [정말, 간절히 badly<br>잘되다 go well] |
| 26 | 난 네가 제일 먼저 알길 바랐어.<br>(네가 제일 먼저 이길 바랐어) | [제일 먼저인<br>the first (to)] |
| 27 | 희망이 있으면 좋겠어. | |
| 28 | 난 종교적이진 않아.<br>하지만 다음 생이 있으면 좋겠어. | [종교적인 religious<br>후생, 다음 생 an afterlife ] |
| 29 | 오늘은 네가 행동 잘하길 바라.<br>(내가 널) 믿어도 되겠어? | [행동 잘하는, 말썽 안 부리는<br>on one's best behavior<br>믿다 count on] |
| 30 | 네가 네 동생한테 잘해주면 좋겠어. | |

기초영어 1000문장 말하기 연습 4

## Speaking Practice (1min)

### 긍정문

☞ 오른쪽 힌트를 이용해서, 직접 문장을 만들어보세요!

| 31 | 네가 행복하길 바라. | |
|---|---|---|
| 32 | 난 그 애가 안전하길 바라. | |
| 33 | 난 그냥 네가 나한테 솔직하면 좋겠어. | [솔직한 honest with] |
| 34 | 네가 용기 내면 좋겠어.<br>(날 위해) 그래 줄 수 있어? | [용기 내는, 용감한, 참는 brave] |
| 35 | 이게 꿈이면 좋겠다.<br>모든 게 원래대로(있던 대로) 돌아갔으면 좋겠어. | [원래대로, 있던 대로 the way it was] |
| 36 | 난 모든 게 완벽하면 좋겠어. | |
| 37 | 내 인생이 더 나았으면 좋겠어.<br>내 인생이 (뭔가) 의미 있길 바라. | [의미 있다 mean] |
| 38 | 모두 다 세상이 더 나아지길 바라.<br>우리는 매일 세상을 더 나은 곳으로 만들고 있어. | |
| 39 | 그 앤 네가 (그의) 여자친구이길 원해. | |
| 40 | 난 그게 그 사람이 길 바랐어.<br>그가 인연이길 바랐어. | [인연, 천생연분,<br>(찾던) 단 한 사람 the one] |

## Speaking Practice (1min)

### 부정문

☞ 오른쪽 힌트를 이용해서, 직접 문장을 만들어보세요!

| | | |
|---|---|---|
| 41 | 네가 안 가면 좋겠어.<br>나랑 같이 있으면 좋겠어. | |
| 42 | 네가 상처받지 않았으면 좋겠어. | [상처받다 get hurt] |
| 43 | 네가 오해하지 않길 바라. | [오해하다<br>get the wrong idea] |
| 44 | 네가 불편한 건 안 했으면 좋겠어.<br>(네가 편안하지 않은 어떤 것이든 하지 않길 바라) | [편안한<br>comfortable with] |
| 45 | 아무한테도 말하지 말아 줄래?<br>내가 여기 있는 거 아무도 몰랐으면 해. | |
| 46 | 난 그 애가 이상한 생각 하지 않았으면 좋겠어.<br>그가 오해하지 않길 바라. | [이상한 생각하다<br>get the wrong idea<br>오해하다 misunderstand] |
| 47 | 난 우리가 더 이상 안 싸웠으면 좋겠어. | [싸우다 fight] |
| 48 | 난 지금 내 모습을 아무에게도 보여주고 싶지 않아.<br>(아무도 이런 나를 보지 않길 바라) | [(지금 모습) 이런<br>like this] |
| 49 | 네가 더 이상의 시간을 낭비하지 않길 바라. | [더 이상의 시간<br>any more time] |
| 50 | 네가 압박감을 느끼지 않았으면 좋겠어. | [압박감 느끼다<br>feel pressured] |

# Speaking Practice 1min

## 부정문

☞ 오른쪽 힌트를 이용해서, 직접 문장을 만들어보세요!

| | | |
|---|---|---|
| 51 | 네가 화내지 않았으면 좋겠어. | |
| 52 | 너 자신을 자책하지 않았으면 좋겠어.<br>아무도 예상하지 못했어. (아무도 그게 오는 걸 보지 않았어) | [자책하는 hard on oneself<br>예상하다 see it coming] |
| 53 | 네가 남의 시선을 (너무) 의식하지 않았으면 좋겠어. | [남의 시선 의식하는<br>self-conscious] |
| 54 | 난 우리가 친구이길 바라지 않아.<br>난 우리가 함께 늙었으면 좋겠어. | [늙다, 나이 들다<br>grow old] |
| 55 | 네가 날 구해줄 필요 없어.<br>내가 (나 자신을) 구할 수 있어. | [구하다 save] |
| 56 | 그게 진실이 아니길 바라. | |
| 57 | 난 네가 완벽하길 바라는 게 아니야.<br>아무도 완벽하지 않아. 난 단지 네가 너 자신이길 바라. | |
| 58 | 너한테 말하고 싶지 않았어.<br>난 네가 너무 마음 상하지 않길 바랐어. | [(너무) 마음 상하다, 불편하다<br>feel bad ] |
| 59 | 난 아무도 모르길 바랐어.<br>(아무도 알길 원하지 않았어) | |
| 60 | 너한테 말 안 했어.<br>네가 걱정하는 게 싫어서. | |

## Speaking Practice 1min

### 부정문 (expect)

☞ 오른쪽 힌트를 이용해서, 직접 문장을 만들어보세요!

| 61 | 난 네가 아무것도 하길 기대하지 않아.<br>네가 하고 싶은 건 뭐든 해. | [뭐든지 whatever] |
|---|---|---|
| 62 | 네가 이해하길 바라지 않아. (기대하지 않아) | |
| 63 | 그가 (날 위해) 이거 해주기를 기대할 수 없어.<br>그는 믿을 만하지 않아. | [믿을만한 reliable] |
| 64 | (우리) 그 애가 모든 일을 다 하기를 기대하지 말아야 해.<br>(기대하지 않는 게 좋겠어) 그는 기계가 아니야. | [모든 일 다 all the work] |
| 65 | 남들이 너와 같기를 기대하지 마. | [남들, 다른 사람<br>other people] |
| 66 | 사람들이 바뀌기를 기대하지 말아야 해.<br>(우린 사람들이 우릴 위해 바뀌길 기대하지 않는 게 좋겠어) | |
| 67 | 난 그 애가 올 줄 몰랐어.<br>(난 그 애가 오는 거 기대하지 않았어) | |
| 68 | 난 아무도 날 도와주길 기대하지 않았어.<br>날 구해줄 사람 필요 없어. (나를 구해줄 아무도 필요 없어) | |
| 69 | 네가 불편한 걸 하길 바라는 사람 없어.<br>(아무도 네가 불편한 걸 하길 기대하지 않아) | |
| 70 | 모두가 널 좋아하길 바라면 안 돼. (기대하면 안 돼)<br>그건 가능하지 않아. | |

# Speaking Practice 1min

## 의문문

☞ 오른쪽 힌트를 이용해서, 직접 문장을 만들어보세요!

| 71 | 내가 같이 가줄까? | [같이 가다 come with] |
|---|---|---|
| 72 | 뭐라도 갖다 줄까? | [가져다주다 get sb some/anything] |
| 73 | 나 가지 말까?<br>(내가 있을까?) | [(가지 않고) 있다 stay] |
| 74 | 내가 운전할까? | |
| 75 | 차 세울까? | [(안전히) 차 세우다 pull over] |
| 76 | 내가 너를 도와주면 좋겠어? | |
| 77 | 네 사진 찍어줄까? | |
| 78 | 택시 불러줄까? | [택시 부르다 call a cab] |
| 79 | 혼내줄까? (내가 뭐라도 할까?)<br>내가 그 애 때려줄까? | [때리다 beat sb up] |
| 80 | 내가 했으면 하는 게 (아무거라도) 있니?<br>내가 뭘 하면 좋겠어? | |

Unit 6

## Speaking Practice 1min

## 의문문

☞ 오른쪽 힌트를 이용해서, 직접 문장을 만들어보세요!

| 81 | 내가 (널 위해) 잠깐 봐줄까? | [잠깐 봐주다, 커버/대신하다 cover for sb] |
|---|---|---|
| 82 | 내가 그 애랑 얘기해 볼까? | |
| 83 | 너 또 그런 일이 생겼으면 좋겠어? | |
| 84 | 모두가 알길 바라는 거야? 그냥 평소대로 행동해. | [평소대로 (행동) 하다 act normal] |
| 85 | 내가 무슨 말을 하길 바라? 내가 뭐라고 말하길 기대하는 거야? 말해줘, 그럼 내가 말할 테니. | |
| 86 | 내가 문자로 주소 보내줄까? | [주소 (문자로) 보내다 text sb the address] |
| 87 | 내가 어떻게 하길 바랐어? (뭘 하길 바랐어?) | |
| 88 | 내가 거짓말하길 바랐어? | |
| 89 | 내가 뭘 하길 바라? (기대해) | |
| 90 | 알았어, 내가 뭘 하면 돼? (내가 뭘 해줄 필요가 있어?) | |

# Speaking Practice
## 1min

### Would you like me to?
☞ 오른쪽 힌트를 이용해서, 직접 문장을 만들어보세요!

| | | |
|---|---|---|
| 91 | 차 좀 (만들어) 줄까요? | [차 (만들어) 주다<br>make sb some tea] |
| 92 | 제가 미팅 주선해 볼까요? | [미팅 주선/계획/준비하다<br>arrange a meeting] |
| 93 | 제가 뭐라도 가져올까요? | |
| 94 | 제가 그거 (널 위해) 해드릴까요? | |
| 95 | 제가 이걸 어떻게 처리했으면 좋겠어요? | [처리하다 handle] |
| 96 | 그만할까요?<br>(멈추길 바라요?) | |
| 97 | 내가 뭐라고 할까?<br>(뭔가 말할까?) | |
| 98 | 링크 보내드릴까요? | [링크 보내다<br>send sb the link] |
| 99 | 그거 어떻게 사용하는 건지 보여줄까요? | |
| 100 | 넌 대단하고, 능력 있고, 엄청난 잠재력을 가지고 있어.<br>더 할까? (계속할까?) | [능력 있는 talented<br>잠재력 있다<br>have (so much) potential<br>계속하다 go on] |

Unit 6

# Review

복습 강의 바로 듣기

| Positive (긍정) | Negative (부정) | Question |
|---|---|---|
| So do I. | Neither do I. | - |
| 나도 | | - |
| Do you? | Don't you? | - |
| 그래? 정말? | | - |
| - | - | Who 동사? What 동사? |
| - | - | 누가? 뭐가? |
| - | - | Don't you? |
| - | - | 안 해? |
| I had p.p. | I hadn't p.p. | Had you p.p.? |
| 했어, 했었어 (그전에) | 안 했어, 안 했었어 | 했어? 했었어? |
| I had been -ing | I hadn't been -ing | Had you been -ing? |
| 했었어 (계속)<br>하고 있었어 | 안 했었어<br>안 하고 있었어 | 했었어?<br>하고 있었어? |
| I want you to | I don't want you to | Do you want me to? |
| 하면 좋겠어, 하길 바라 | 안 하면 좋겠어 | 할까? 하면 좋겠어? |

# help & can't help it

배운 내용을 생각하며, 직접 문장을 만들어보세요!

정답확인 : P 267

| 01 | 우리가 그를 도와주는 게 좋을 것 같아. |
|---|---|
| 02 | 네가 그 애한테 부탁하면 도와줄 거야. |
| 03 | 내가 너의 그 프로젝트를 도와줄 수 있어.<br>-그래줄 수 있어? 고마워. |
| 04 | 너 나 도와줘야 돼. |
| 05 | (요즘) 엄마 장 보는 거 도와드리고 있어. [장보기 돕다 help sb with groceries] |
| 06 | 미안. 난 단지 도우려는 거였어. [도우려고 하다 try to help] |
| 07 | 엄청난 도움이 되었어.(넌 엄청나게 날 도왔어) 정말 고마워.<br>[엄청나게, 대단하게 immensely] |
| 08 | 난 그거 혼자 하지 않았어. 내 친구가 도와줬어. |
| 09 | 내가 (너) 그거 도와주려고 했었는데. |
| 10 | 알아. (그거) 소화에 도움 돼. 도움 많이 돼. [~에 도움 되다 help with 소화 digestion]<br>-그래? |
| 11 | 이거 물이랑 먹어. 너 머리 아픈 거에 도움 될 거야. [(약) 먹다 take] |
| 12 | 그게 네가 자는 데 도움이 될 수도 있어. 해보는 게 어때? [(~하는데) 도움 되다 help sb] |
| 13 | 규칙적인 운동은 네가 우울을 극복하는 데 도움이 될 거야.<br>[규칙적인 운동 regular exercise 우울을 극복하다 overcome depression] |
| 14 | 넌 내가 널 도와주길 바라지? |
| 15 | 난 그냥 돕고 싶었어. |

# Review

| | |
|---|---|
| 16 | 때로는 모두 도움이 필요해. 내가 널 도울 수 있게 (허락) 하는 게 어때?<br>[돕게 (허락) 하다 let-help] |
| 17 | (너 날) 안 도와줘도 돼. 내가 알아서 할 수 있어. [알아서 (처리) 하다, 해내다 manage] |
| 18 | 미안해, 널 도와주지 못했어서. |
| 19 | 그건 수면에 방해될 거야. (그건 내가 잠자는 걸 돕지 않을 거야) |
| 20 | 내가 방해하는 거지? (내가 도움이 안 되고 있지, 그렇지?) 미안, 비켜줄게.<br>[비키다 get out of one's way] |
| 21 | 난 누구의 도움도 바라지 않아. (난 아무도 날 돕지 않았으면 좋겠어)<br>혼자(스스로) 할 수 있어. |
| 22 | 그 애도 예전엔 집안일을 도와주지 않았었어. [집안일 돕다 help around the house] |
| 23 | 그건 도움 안 돼.<br>-그러니? |
| 24 | 그건 전혀 도움이 안 됐어. 오히려 더 악화시켰어. (그건 그걸 심지어 더 나쁘게 만들었어)<br>[악화시키다 make sth (even) worse] |
| 25 | 안타깝지만 (유감이지만) 널 도와줄 수가 없어. |
| 26 | 그 애가 처음으로 쓰레기를 내다 버렸어. 전에는 도와준 적이 없었어.<br>[쓰레기 버리다 take out the trash 처음으로 for the first time] |
| 27 | 우리가 그 애를 어떻게 도울 수 있는지 모르겠어. |
| 28 | 나 이것 좀 도와줄래? |
| 29 | 내가 (너) 그거 도와줄까? |
| 30 | 너희 남편은 집안일 도와? |

## help & can't help it

배운 내용을 생각하며, 직접 문장을 만들어보세요!

| 31 | 그게 도움이 되었어? |
|----|----|
| 32 | (너) 날 도와주려고는 했었어? 언제 그러려고 했어? |
| 33 | 그게 도움이 돼? |
| 34 | 그게 도움이 될 거 같아? |
| 35 | 우리가 어떻게 돕는 게 좋을 것 같아? |
| 36 | 나 도와줄 거야, 말 거야? |
| 37 | 왜 아무도 그를 돕지 않았어? |
| 38 | 변비에 뭐가 좋을까? (뭐가 도움 될까?) [변비 constipation] |
| 39 | 누가 널 도와줬어? 누가 그랬는지 알아? |
| 40 | 웃으면 안 되는 거 아는데. (웃지 않는 게 좋은 거 아는데) **어쩔 수가 없어.**<br>[어쩔 수가 없어, 못 참겠어, 하지 않을 수 없다 I can't help it.] |
| 41 | 그만 먹어야 되는데. (더 이상 먹지 않는 게 좋겠는데) **참을 수가 없어.** |
| 42 | 계속 슬퍼. (슬픈 감정을 어쩔 수가 없어) |
| 43 | 실례지만, 대화하는 걸 우연히 들었는데요. (너희 대화를 안 들을 수가 없었어요)<br>[우연히 듣다, 엿듣다 overhear 대화 conversation] |
| 44 | 널 쳐다보지 않을 수가 없었어. (널 눈치채지 않을 수 없었어) **넌 정말 아름다워.**<br>[눈치채다, 보다, 주목하다 notice] |
| 45 | 내가 측은하다는 마음이 계속 들었어. (나 자신이 불쌍한 마음을 어쩔 수가 없었어)<br>[불쌍, 측은하다 (자기 연민) feel sorry for oneself] |

# Dialogue Practice

## My wishes for you

I want you to be happy, because you deserve it.

I want you to be healthy, because health is wealth.

I want you to love the people around you, because love is so precious.

I want you to believe in yourself, because you have so much potential.

I want you to dream big, because anything is possible.

I want your worries to stay small, because worrying will never change the outcome.

I want you to enjoy every moment of your life, because life is too short.

I want your life to be all that you want it to be!

# Dialogue Practice

**My wishes for you**

네가 행복하길 바라, 넌 그럴 자격이 있으니까. [충분히 누릴 자격 있다, 받을만하다 deserve]

네가 건강하길 바라, 건강이 재산이니까. [건강 health 재산, 부 wealth]

네 주변 사람들을 사랑하면 좋겠어, 사랑은 정말 소중하니까.
[주변 사람 the people around sb 소중한 precious]

너 자신을 믿으면 좋겠어, 넌 정말 많은 잠재력이 있으니까.
[믿다 believe in 잠재력 (so much) potential]

네가 큰 꿈을 꾸길 바라, 무엇이든 가능하니까.
[큰 꿈을 꾸다 dream big 무엇이든, 어떤 것이든 anything]

네 걱정들은 작게 남으면 좋겠어, 걱정(하는 것)은 결코 결과를 바꾸지 못하니까. [걱정들 worries 걱정 (하는 것) worrying 결과 outcome]

네 인생의 모든 순간을 즐기길 바라, 인생은 너무 짧으니까.
[인생의 모든 순간 every moment of one's life]

난 네 인생이 네가 원하는 대로 되길 바라. (네 인생이 네가 원하는 그대로 모두 되길 바라) [네가 원하는 그대로 모두 all that you want it to be]

# Unit

# 7

누군가 (하라고) 한말을
전달하고 싶을 때

## Unit 7
### 누군가 (하라고) 한말을 전달하고 싶을 때

# I told you to "하라고 했어"

일상 대화에서 우리는, 누군가 한 말을 전달하는 경우가 생각보다 정말 많아요! 그럴 때 사용하는 간접화법, 첫 번째 파트입니다. 간단하게, 누군가가 "하라고" 혹은 "하지 말라고" 했던 말이나 요청, 혹은 부탁들을 다시 전달할 때 "told-to" 를 사용해요!

| Positive | | Negative | Question |
|---|---|---|---|
| I told you to | I told you not to | I didn't tell you to | Did you tell me to? |
| 하라고 했어 | 하지 말라고 했어 | 하라고 안 했어 | 하라고 했어? |

보통 "하라고" 한 말들은 짧게 의미만을 전달한 경우로, 동사를 바로 넣어 명령문 (3권 1단원)을 사용했거나, "Can you?" 등을 사용한 부탁의 경우가 많아요. 그래서 "told" 이외에도 "asked" 역시도 정말 많이 사용해요!

> 이렇게 만듭니다!

"주인공 told 누군가 + (not) to 동사원형"

I told you to / I told you not to 뒤에 동사 원형을 넣어주면 돼요!

| 긍정 | 부정 | 부정 | 의문 |
|---|---|---|---|
| He told me to go.<br>(나 보고) 가래. | He told me not to go.<br>(나 보고) 가지 말래. | He didn't tell me to go.<br>가라고 안 했어. | Did you tell me to go?<br>가라고 했어? |

**<간접화법에서 자주 사용되는 동사들>**

| tell | 말하다, 말해주다 |
|---|---|
| ask | 부탁하다, 물어보다 |
| advise | 조언하다 |
| teach | 가르쳐 주다 |
| order | 명령하다 |
| beg | 애원하다, 빌다 |
| force | 강요하다 |
| warn | 하지 말라고 하다, 위험하다고 하다 |

## 긍정문

☞ 오른쪽 힌트를 이용해서, 직접 문장을 만들어보세요!

정답확인 : P 268

| 01 | 내가 그 애한테 서두르라고 했어.<br>금방 내려올 거야. | [내려오는 down<br>금방, 곧 in a minute] |
|----|----|----|
| 02 | Tim이 나 보고 그거 읽어보라고 했어.<br>읽어봤는데, 난 너무 좋았어. | |
| 03 | 내가 Tim 보고 와서 우리 픽업하라고 했어.<br>곧 여기 올 거야. | |
| 04 | Tim 이 방금 전화했었어.<br>우리한테 전화 다시 하라고 말했어. | |
| 05 | 내가 너한테 그거 가져오라고 했잖아, 그렇지? | |
| 06 | 그가 우리 보고 자기를 따라오래. | |
| 07 | 내가 너한테 이것들 치우라고 했잖아.<br>왜 아직 안 했어? | [치우다, 제자리 놓다<br>put-away] |
| 08 | 내가 너한테 그거 해보라고 했잖아. | |
| 09 | 내가 Sarah한테 한 시간 전에 준비하라고 했어.<br>그 앤 준비하는데 왜 이렇게 오래 걸리는 거지? | |
| 10 | 우리가 그에게 그거 가져가라고 했어.<br>그래서, 그 애가 그거 가지고 있어. | |

# Speaking Practice
## 1min

### 긍정문
☞ 오른쪽 힌트를 이용해서, 직접 문장을 만들어보세요!

| | | |
|---|---|---|
| 11 | 네가 나 보고 이거 하라며.<br>그래서 했는데.<br>🔊 | [그래서~다, 그게~한 이유다<br>That's why] |
| 12 | 그 애가 나 보고 여기서 기다리랬어.<br>그래서 여기서 기다리는 거야.<br>🔊 | |
| 13 | 내가 그 애 보고 그거 가지라고 했어.<br>그래서 그 애가 가지고 있는 거야.<br>🔊 | |
| 14 | 네가 나 보고 거기 가라며.<br>그래서 거기 갔던 건데.<br>🔊 | |
| 15 | 네가 나 보고 그 애한테 말하라고 했잖아.<br>그래서 말한 거야.<br>🔊 | |
| 16 | Jim이 나 보고 와달라고 (부탁) 했어.<br>그래서 온 거야.<br>🔊 | |
| 17 | Kim이 이걸 해달라고 했어.<br>그래서 이거 하는 거야.<br>🔊 | |
| 18 | 네가 이거 사라며.<br>그래서 산 건데.<br>🔊 | |
| 19 | 그가 우리 보고 제목을 바꾸라고 했어.<br>그래서 또다시 바꾸고 있는 거야.<br>🔊 | [제목 the title] |
| 20 | 그 앤 항상 나 자신을 믿고 목표를 달성하도록 격려해 줬어.<br>그래서 내가 그 앨 존경하는 거야.<br>🔊 | [격려하다 encourage<br>믿다 believe in<br>달성하다, 이루다 achieve ] |

# Speaking Practice 1min

## 긍정문

☞ 오른쪽 힌트를 이용해서, 직접 문장을 만들어보세요!

| | | |
|---|---|---|
| 21 | 내가 그에게 도와달라고 부탁했어.<br>도움이 절실히 필요해.<br>(우리가 얻을 수 있는 모든 도움이 필요해) | [모든 도움 all the help<br>얻다, 구하다 get] |
| 22 | Sean이 내게 널 잘 챙겨달라고 부탁했어. | [잘 챙기다, 신경 쓰다<br>look out for sb] |
| 23 | 난 그에게 있어 달라고 부탁했어.<br>혼자 있고 싶지 않았어. | |
| 24 | 그가 나보고 너랑 같이 있어주래.<br>그 앤 널 정말 좋아해. (널 정말 신경 써) | [정말 좋아하다, 신경 쓰다<br>care about ] |
| 25 | 네가 이거 달라며.<br>이게 네가 가장 좋아하는 거라는 거 알아. | |
| 26 | 그가 그녀에게 결혼해 달라고 했어.<br>그들은 다음 달에 결혼할 거야. | [~와 결혼하다 marry<br>결혼(식) 하다 get married] |
| 27 | 내가 그에게 조용히 하라고 했어. | |
| 28 | 그는 내게 자연스럽게 하라고 했어.<br>(평소 모습 그대로 나답게) | [자연스럽게/평소대로/자신답<br>게 하다 be oneself] |
| 29 | 내가 그 애들한테 조심하라고 했어.<br>난 그들이 너무 걱정됐어. | |
| 30 | 내가 너보고 그 애한테 잘해주라고 했잖아.<br>내가 딱 하나 해달라고 부탁한 건데, 넌 그것도 못했어. | [잘해주는 nice to sb<br>딱하나 one thing] |

# Speaking Practice 1min

## 긍정문

☞ 오른쪽 힌트를 이용해서, 직접 문장을 만들어보세요!

| | | |
|---|---|---|
| 31 | 그 애가 나보고 너한테 물어보랬어.<br>도와줄 수 있어? | |
| 32 | 그 애가 나보고 내려놓으라는데.<br>그래야 되는 거 알지만, 너무 힘들다. | [내려놓다 let go] |
| 33 | 그들은 점점 불안해했어.<br>내가 조급해하지 말라고 했어. (참으라고 했어) | [불안/조급해지다 get anxious<br>조급해하지 마, 참다, 인내하다<br>be patient] |
| 34 | 그 애가 참견하더라고.<br>네 일이나 잘하라고 했어. | [오지랖 부리는, 참견하는 nosy<br>자기일 이나 잘하다, 신경쓰다<br>mind one's own business] |
| 35 | 네가 나보고 (뭔가) 새로운 거 해보라고 했잖아.<br>좋은 조언이었어. | |
| 36 | 그 애가 나보고 너한테 말해주래.<br>그 애가 널 진짜 좋아하는 것 같아. | |
| 37 | 내가 그 애 보고 우리한테 시간을 더 달라고 했어. | |
| 38 | 그 애가 나 보고 하나를 고르라고 했어.<br>난 어떤 걸 고르고 싶은지 모르겠어. | [고르다 choose, pick] |
| 39 | 네가 나 보고 내가 원하는 거 아무거나 사라며.<br>내가 너무 많이 썼어? | [(돈) 쓰다 spend<br>너무 많이 too much] |
| 40 | (그들은) 모두 내게 그걸 무시해 버리라고 했지.<br>하지만 그게 바로 네 눈앞에 있을 땐 쉽지 않아. | [바로, 딱, 정확히 right<br>눈/얼굴 앞에 in one's face] |

# Speaking Practice 1min

## 긍정문

☞ 오른쪽 힌트를 이용해서, 직접 문장을 만들어보세요!

| | | |
|---|---|---|
| 41 | 그 애 그거에 대해 확신이 없어 보여서,<br>내가 생각해 보라고 했어. | [확신 없어 보이다, 망설이다<br>seem unsure] |
| 42 | 그 애가 나보고 내 직감을 믿으랬어.<br>난 이번 건 내 직감을 따를 거야. | [직감을 믿다<br>trust one's instinct<br>직감/촉 따르다<br>go with one's gut (on)] |
| 43 | 그가 나에게 이거 하는 법을 가르쳐 줬어. | |
| 44 | 그가 그녀에게 다시 받아달라고 애원했어.<br>그 후에 어떻게 됐는지는 모르겠어.<br>(무슨 일이 생겼는지는 몰라) | [빌다, 애원하다 beg<br>다시 받아주다 take sb back] |
| 45 | 그 애가 내게 그거 알아봐 달라고 부탁했어. | [알아보다, 조사하다<br>look into] |
| 46 | 그가 내가 준비될 때까지 기다리라고 (조언) 했어. | |
| 47 | 그 애가 일자리 제의를 수락하라고 설득했어.<br>그 애가 꼬셨어. | [설득하다 persuade<br>설득하다, 꼬시다 talk sb into] |
| 48 | 의사가 그에게 살을 빼라고 (조언) 했어. | [살 빼다 lose weight] |
| 49 | 의사가 너 보고 운동을 하라고 했잖아.<br>그의 말 들을 필요가 있어. | |
| 50 | 의사가 그 애 보고 담배 끊으라고 했어.<br>그리고 그는 작년 4월에 담배 끊었어. | [담배 끊다<br>quit/give up smoking] |

## Speaking Practice  1min

### 긍정문

☞ 오른쪽 힌트를 이용해서, 직접 문장을 만들어보세요.

| | | |
|---|---|---|
| 51 | 내가 그거 하지 말라고 했지? (그렇지?) | |
| 52 | 그 애가 나 보고 가지 말라고 (부탁) 했어. | |
| 53 | 가만히 있어.<br>그 애가 우리 보고 움직이지 말라고 했어. | [가만히 있다 keep still] |
| 54 | 내가 모르는 사람이랑 이야기하지 말라고 했잖아. | [모르는 사람 strangers] |
| 55 | 내가 웃지 말라고 했잖아.<br>그만해! 나 진지해. | |
| 56 | 그 애가 우리 보고 기다리지 말라고 했어.<br>그 애 늦을 거야. | |
| 57 | 내가 그건 걱정하지 말라고 했잖아.<br>걱정할 필요 없어. | |
| 58 | 그 애가 우리 보고 서두르지 말라고 했어.<br>천천히 하라고 했어. | [천천히 하다<br>take one's time] |
| 59 | 의사가 우리한테 창문 열지 말라고 했어.<br>따뜻하게 해야 돼. | [따뜻하게 (유지) 하다<br>keep warm] |
| 60 | 그 애가 나한테 고기 먹지 말래. | |

# Speaking Practice 1min

## 긍정문
☞ 오른쪽 힌트를 이용해서, 직접 문장을 만들어보세요!

| | | |
|---|---|---|
| 61 | 그 애가 희망을 잃지 말라고 했는데.<br>하지만 난 희망이 없어. (희망 없는 느낌이야) | [희망 없는, 절망적인<br>hoepless] |
| 62 | 네가 오늘 오지 말라며.<br>기억 안 나? | |
| 63 | 내가 아무한테도 말하지 말아 달라고 했잖아.<br>네가 왜 그에게 말했는지 이해가 안 돼. | |
| 64 | 나보고 아무 말도 하지 말아달라며.<br>아무 말도 안 할 거야. | |
| 65 | Jim이 우리 보고 이거 쓰지 말랬어.<br>우리 이거 안 쓰는 게 좋겠어. | |
| 66 | 내가 그 애 믿지 말라고 (경고) 했잖아.<br>그 애는 바람둥이야. | [경고하다 warn<br>바람둥이 a cheater] |
| 67 | 그 애들이랑 어울리지 말라고 했잖아. | [어울리다, 놀다<br>hang out with] |
| 68 | 그에게 다시는 나한테 연락하지 말라고 했어. | [연락하다 contact] |
| 69 | 그 애한테 거짓말하지 말라고 했는데.<br>난 거짓말 싫어. | |
| 70 | 그 애가 나 보고 가지 말아 달라고 빌었어.<br>그를 떠나기 정말 힘들었어. | [빌다, 애원하다 beg] |

## Speaking Practice 1min

### 긍정문

☞ 오른쪽 힌트를 이용해서, 직접 문장을 만들어보세요!

| | | |
|---|---|---|
| 71 | 네가 방해하지 말라며.<br>그래서 아까 너한테 말하지 않은 거야. | [방해하다 bother] |
| 72 | 그 애한테 자랑하지 말라고 했어.<br>그 앤 자기 자랑을 많이 해. (자랑쟁이야) | [자랑하다 brag<br>자랑쟁이 (such) a show-off] |
| 73 | 그 애가 변화를 두려워하지 말라고 했는데. | |
| 74 | 그 애가 그거 무서워하지 말라고 했어.<br>공포를 직면하라고 했어. | [공포/두려움을 마주/직면하다<br>face one's fears] |
| 75 | 그 애가 우리 보고 늦지 말랬어.<br>우리 곧 나가는 게 좋겠어. | |
| 76 | 내가 너 그거 하지 말라고 (경고) 했잖아. | |
| 77 | 네가 아무것도 바꾸지 말라며. | |
| 78 | 그 애 보고 이거 망치지 말라고 했어. | [망치다 ruin] |
| 79 | 그 애가 까먹지 말라고 했는데. | |
| 80 | 나 일하는 동안 방해하지 말라고 했잖아.<br>뭐가 그렇게 급해? | [방해하다, 끊다<br>interrupt] |

Unit 7

# Speaking Practice
## 1min

### 부정문
☞ 오른쪽 힌트를 이용해서, 직접 문장을 만들어보세요!

| | | |
|---|---|---|
| 81 | 너 보고 나 기다리라고 하지 않았잖아.<br>기다리지 않아도 됐는데. | |
| 82 | 그 애한테 그거 하라고 하지 않았어.<br>무슨 이야기하는 거야? | |
| 83 | 난 그 애한테 도와달라고 하지 않았어. | |
| 84 | 그 애가 우리한테 그거 가져오라고 하지 않았는데.<br>그거 가져왔어야 돼? | |
| 85 | 난 너한테 아무것도 해달라고 하지 않았어. | |
| 86 | 내가 너한테 이거 하라고 하지 않았네.<br>미안, 그 말 한다는 거 깜박했어. | [말하다, 언급하다]<br>mention |
| 87 | 그 애가 나 보고 전화하라고 하지 않았어.<br>그 애가 먼저 전화할 때까지 전화 안 할 거야. | |
| 88 | 그 애가 나한테 오라고 강요하지 않았어.<br>내가 여기 오고 싶었어. | [강요하다 force] |
| 89 | 아무도 나한테 이거 하라고 강요하지 않았어.<br>내 결정이었어. 내가 다 책임질게. (내가 모든 책임을 져) | [모든 책임을 지다]<br>take full responsibility |
| 90 | 아무도 이거 (하는 거) 나한테 가르쳐 주지 않았어.<br>그거 독학했어. (스스로 배운 거였어) | [독학인, 스스로 배운]<br>self-taught |

# Speaking Practice
## 1min

## 의문문

☞ 오른쪽 힌트를 이용해서, 직접 문장을 만들어보세요!

| | | |
|---|---|---|
| 91 | 네가 그 애 보고 가라고 했어?<br>왜 그랬어? | |
| 92 | 그럼, 나 보고 왜 그거 하라고 한 거야? | |
| 93 | 내가 너한테 언제 그러라고 했어? | |
| 94 | 그 애가 네게 뭘 하라고 (조언) 했어? | |
| 95 | 말해줘. 내가 너한테 뭐 해달라고 했지? | |
| 96 | 내가 너 보고 오늘 오라고 했었나? | |
| 97 | 너 방금 나한테 도와달라고 (부탁) 한 거야? | |
| 98 | 내가 너한테 그거 하지 말라고 몇 번을 말했어? | |
| 99 | 누가 너 보고 그거 하라고 했어? | |
| 100 | 나 보고 2시까지 오라고 하지 않았어? | |

# Review

| Positive (긍정) | | Negative (부정) | Question |
|---|---|---|---|
| So do I. | | Neither do I. | - |
| 나도 | | | - |
| Do you? | | Don't you? | - |
| 그래? 정말? | | | - |
| - | | - | Who 동사? What 동사? |
| - | | - | 누가? 뭐가? |
| - | | - | Don't you? |
| - | | - | 안 해? |
| I had p.p. | | I hadn't p.p. | Had you p.p.? |
| 했어, 했었어 (그전에) | | 안 했어, 안 했었어 | 했어? 했었어? |
| I had been -ing | | I hadn't been -ing | Had you been -ing? |
| 했었어 (계속)<br>하고 있었어 | | 안 했었어<br>안 하고 있었어 | 했었어?<br>하고 있었어? |
| I want you to | | I don't want you to | Do you want me to? |
| 하면 좋겠어, 하길 바라 | | 안 하면 좋겠어 | 할까? 하면 좋겠어? |
| I told you to | I told you not to | I didn't tell you to | Did you tell me to? |
| 하래<br>하라고 했어 | 하지 말래<br>하지 말라고 했어 | 하라고 안 했어 | 하라고 했어? |

# try & worth a try

배운 내용을 생각하며, 직접 문장을 만들어보세요!

정답확인 : P 271

| 01 | (너) 이거 해봐도 돼. |
|---|---|
| 02 | 나 새로운 취미를 시도해 볼지도 몰라. |
| 03 | 제가 나중에 다시 해볼게요. |
| 04 | 난 새로운 거 시도하는 게 좋아. [새로운 것들 new things] |
| 05 | 네가 노력 많이 한 거 알아. [노력 (많이) 하다 try hard] |
| 06 | 다 해봤어. (난 모든 걸 시도해 봤어) |
| 07 | 해봤는데, 안돼. (나 그거 해봤는데, 안됐어) |
| 08 | (뭔가) 다른 거 시도해 보고 있었어. [다른 거 something different] |
| 09 | 해봐. (너 그거 해보는 게 좋겠어) |
| 10 | 내가 더 노력해야겠지? [더 노력하다 try harder] |
| 11 | 나라면 최선을 다하겠어. [최선을 다하다 try one's best] |
| 12 | 우리 여기 있는 김에 해보지 뭐. (우리 여기 있는 동안에 그거 해보지 뭐) |
| 13 | 그 애가 그렇게 되게 만들려고 노력하고 있어. 그리고 나도. [되게 하다/만들다 make-work] |
| 14 | (뭔가) 새로운 거 해보고 싶어. [새로운 거 something new] |
| 15 | 이거 해보라며. (네가 나 이거 해보라고 했잖아) -그랬나? |

Unit 7

# Review

| | |
|---|---|
| 16 | 네가 이거 해봤으면 좋겠어. |
| 17 | 노력하고 있어. [노력하다 try] |
| 18 | 더 이상은 노력하고 싶지 않아. |
| 19 | (그거) 처음이었어. 전에 해본 적 없어. (전에 안 해봤어) |
| 20 | 노력이 부족해. (넌 충분히 노력하고 있지 않아) [충분히 (노력하는) hard enough] |
| 21 | 우리 그건 아직 안 해봤다. |
| 22 | 뭘 하려던 게 아니야. (아무것도 하려고 하지 않았어) [하려고 하다 try to] |
| 23 | 그 앤 더 이상 노력하지 않아. |
| 24 | 널 막으려는 게 아니야. (널 막으려고 하는 게 아니야) |
| 25 | 집에서는 따라 하지 마세요. (이걸 집에서 시도하지 마세요) |
| 26 | 멍청한 짓 하지 말고. (멍청한 짓 시도하지 않는 게 좋겠어) [멍청한 짓 anything stupid] |
| 27 | 이거 해볼래? |
| 28 | 이거 해봐도 돼? |
| 29 | 나 이거 해보는 게 좋을 거 같아? |
| 30 | 내가 이거 해볼까? (넌 내가 이걸 해보길 바라?) |

## try & worth a try

배운 내용을 생각하며, 직접 문장을 만들어보세요!

| 31 | 뭐 하는 거야? (너 뭘 하려고 하는 거야?) |
| --- | --- |
| 32 | 뭐 하려는 거였어? (뭘 하려고 하고 있었어?) |
| 33 | 이거 해본 적 있어? |
| 34 | 그건 해봤어? |
| 35 | 그거 해보는 게 어때? |
| 36 | 너 그거 해볼 거야? |
| 37 | 너 그거 시도해 볼 거 같아? |
| 38 | 무슨 말 하려는 거야? |
| 39 | 네가 나 이거 해보라고 하지 않았어? |
| 40 | 그는 왜 자살하려고 했던 거야? [자살하려고 하다 try to kill oneself] |
| 41 | 노력을 왜 해? (왜 애를 써?) 왜 굳이? (왜 귀찮게?) [귀찮게 하다 bother] |
| 42 | 넌 이해 못 할 거야. (너라면 이해하지 않을 거야)<br>-한번 말해봐! [한번 말해봐, 난 다를 수 있어, 날 시험해 봐 Try me!] |
| 43 | 아무도 날 믿지 않을걸.<br>-한번 말해봐. 난 그럴 수도. (난 믿을지도 몰라) |
| 44 | 그거 해봐라. (너 그거 해보는 게 좋겠어) 해볼 만한 가치가 있어.<br>[해볼 만한 가치 있는 worth a try] |
| 45 | 음, 그건 해볼 만한 가치가 있었어. 시도해 봤어야 했어. |

# Dialogue Practice

**I told you so!**

**A**: What did you do last night?

**B**: I went out with Jim.
I know you told me not to go out last night.

**A**: Yes, you were not feeling well.
And I also told you not to hang out with Jim.

**B**: Anyway, Jim begged me to go to the concert with him, and I couldn't refuse.

**A**: So, how was the concert?

**B**: It was terrible. I couldn't enjoy the music because I wasn't feeling too well.
I just wanted to get out of there.
And on top of that, my cold got worse.

**A**: I told you so!

**A**: What did I tell you? I told you not to do that.

**B**: Yeah, yeah. I know. Everyone told me to be careful.

**A**: Yes, it sounded too good to be true.
I warned you not to do that. Why didn't you listen to me?

**B**: I don't know. I wanted it to work.
I wanted to believe it to be true.

**A**: I hate to say this, but I told you so.

**B**: You don't hate to say it, do you?

**A**: Yes, I do! I didn't want to be right.

**B**: But why are you smiling? You're enjoying this, aren't you?

**A**: No, I'm not. Sorry, I'll stop saying I told you so.

# Dialogue Practice

**I told you so!**

그러게 내가 뭐랬어! (꼴좋다, 쌤통이다)

**A:** 어젯밤에 뭐 했어?

**B:** Jim이랑 밖에 나갔었어.
어젯밤에 네가 나가지 말라고 한거 아는데.

**A:** 어, 너 몸이 좀 안 좋았었잖아. [몸이 안 좋다 (not) feel well]
그리고 내가 Jim이랑 어울리지 말라고도 말했잖아.
[~도, 또한 also 어울리다 hang out with]

**B:** 어쨌든, Jim이 (그랑) 같이 콘서트 가자고 사정해서,
거절할 수가 없었어. [사정/애원하다 beg, 거절하다 refuse]

**A:** 그래서, 콘서트는 어땠어?

**B:** 끔찍했어. 음악을 즐길 수 없었어, 몸이 너무 안 좋아서.
난 그냥 거기서 벗어나고 싶었어. [벗어나다, 나오다 get out of]
게다가, 내 감기가 더 나빠졌어. [게다가, 그에 더해서 on top of that]

**A:** 그러게 내가 뭐랬어!

A: 내가 너한테 뭐라 그랬어? 그거 하지 말라고 했잖아.

B: 그래, 그래. 알아. 모두 나한테 조심하라고 했지.

A: 어, (그 소리가) 말도 안 되게 좋아 보이더라고. (들리더라고)
   [말도 안 되게 좋은, 사실이라고 믿기 힘들 정도로 좋은 too good to be true]
   내가 그거 하지 말라고 (경고) 했잖아. 왜 내 말을 안 들었어?

B: 몰라. 난 그게 되길 바랐어. 난 그게 사실이라고 믿고 싶었어.

A: 이런 말은 하기 싫지만, 그러게 내가 뭐랬어.

B: 그 말, 하기 싫은 거 아니지?

A: 맞아! (싫어) 내가 맞기를 바라지 않았어.

B: 근데 그 미소는 뭐야? (왜 웃고 있어?) 너 즐기고 있지?

A: 아니야. 미안해. 그러게 내가 뭐랬어, 라고 그만 말할게.

# Unit

# 8

누군가 했던 말을
전달하고 싶을 때

## Unit 8
### 누군가 했던 말을 전달하고 싶을 때

# I said (that) "했다고 했어"

간접화법 두 번째 파트는 누군가 "했던" 말을 전달할 때의 경우에요. 지난 단원에서는, 짧게 의미만을 전달하는 명령문이나 부탁을 위주로 해서, **동사**만 연결하면 되었는데요. 이번 단원에서는 누군가 "했었던 말 자체", **문장**을 전달할 때 사용하는 표현들이에요.

| Positive (긍정) | Negative (부정) | Question (의문) |
|---|---|---|
| I said (that) <br> I told you (that) | I didn't say (that) <br> I didn't tell you (that) | Did you say (that)? <br> Did you tell me (that)? |
| 했다고 했어 | 했다고 하지 않았어 | 했다고 했어? |

"say" 나 "tell" 을 사용할 수 있고요. 뒤에 문장을 연결할 것이라 "that" 을 넣어도 되고, 생략도 가능합니다.

간접화법의 경우는 이미 했던 말의 전달이라서, 거의 과거형 동사 "said" 나 "told" 를 사용해요. 그래서 당연히, 뒤에 연결되는 문장 역시도 과거형으로 나와요!!!

### 이렇게 만듭니다!

I said (that) + 과거 문장

시제를 맞추어 동일하게 과거 문장들이 나와야 해서, 원래 말했던
문장의 **시제가 뒤로 물러나게 돼요!** 또한, 주인공도 자연스럽게 바뀝니다!

| 시제 | | | 직접화법 | 간접화법 |
|---|---|---|---|---|
| am, is, are | ⇨ | was, were | "I am hungry." | He said he was hungry. |
| 현재 | ⇨ | 과거 | "I like it." | He said he liked it. |
| 과거 | ⇨ | 과거완료 | "I made it." | He said he had made it. |
| 현재완료 | ⇨ | 과거완료 | "I have been there." | He said he had been there. |
| will | ⇨ | would | "I'll do it." | He said he would do it. |
| can | ⇨ | could | "I can do it." | He said he could do it. |

**<시제 변환의 예외>**

상대가 했던 그 말이 늘 진실이고, 사실인 경우는 시제를 뒤로 변환할 필요 없
이 현재 그대로 사용해도 좋아요!

**<비교>**

| 간접화법 1 (7단원) | 간접화법 2 (8단원) |
|---|---|
| 누군가 **(하라고) 한 말**의 전달<br>-**"to"** + 동사 원형 | 누군가 **했던 말**의 전달<br>-**"문장"** 연결 |
| He told me to do it.<br>(그 애가 나 보고 이거 하래. (하라고 했어) | He told me he had done it.<br>그 애 그거 했대. (했다고 말했어) |

**<시간의 변화>**

| 직접화법 | ⇨ | 간접화법 | 직접화법 | ⇨ | 간접화법 |
|---|---|---|---|---|---|
| now | ⇨ | now, then | tomorrow | ⇨ | tomorrow, the following/next day |
| this | ⇨ | this, that | yesterday | ⇨ | yesterday, the day before |

# 긍정문

☞ 오른쪽 힌트를 이용해서, 직접 문장을 만들어보세요!

정답확인 : P 272

| 01 | 그 애가 이거 좋대.<br>나도 그렇게 생각해. (난 그 애 의견에 동의해) | [동의하다 agree with ] |
|---|---|---|
| 02 | 그 애가 36살이라고 했어.<br>난 그 애한테 그 나이로 안 보인다고 말했어. | [제 나이로 보이다<br>look one's age] |
| 03 | 내 친구 중의 한 명이 그러는데 이 책 좋대.<br>나한테 추천해 줬어. | [추천하다<br>recommend-to] |
| 04 | 내가 너한테 이건 너무 작다고 했잖아.<br>우리는 더 큰 게 필요해. | [더 큰 거<br>something bigger] |
| 05 | 그 애가 급하댔어.<br>지금 전화해 봐. (전화하는 게 좋겠어) | |
| 06 | 내가 미안하다고 했잖아.<br>나한테 더 이상 뭘 바라? (원해) | [더 이상 뭘, 뭘 더<br>what more] |
| 07 | 너 배고프다며.<br>왜 안 먹어? | |
| 08 | 그 애가 그거 어렵댔어. | |
| 09 | 그 애가 말하길, 네가 많은 도움이 된다고 하더라.<br>도와줘서 고마워. | [도움 되는 helpful] |
| 10 | 그들이 (그게) 다음 주 토요일이라고 했지, 그렇지? | |

## 긍정문

☞ 오른쪽 힌트를 이용해서, 직접 문장을 만들어보세요!

| 11 | 그 애가 그거 공짜라고 했는데. 🔊 | |
| --- | --- | --- |
| 12 | 그 애 실망했대. 마음이 불편해.<br>내가 그 앨 실망시켰어. 🔊 | [마음 불편하다, 미안하다 feel so bad<br>실망시키다 let-down] |
| 13 | 모두 그걸 하는 게 불가능하다고 말했어.<br>하지만 난 신경 쓰지 않았어. 🔊 | [신경 쓰다 care] |
| 14 | 네가 그거 실수라며.<br>실수였지? 🔊 | |
| 15 | 내가 너한테 그건 너무 늦었다고 했잖아. 🔊 | |
| 16 | 그 애가 거기서 불행하다고 했어.<br>일 그만두고 싶다고 나한테 말했어. 🔊 | [그만두다 quit] |
| 17 | 내가 아무것도 걱정할 거 없다고 그 애한테 말했어. 🔊 | |
| 18 | Carol이 문제 없다고 했어.<br>그리고 난 그 앨 믿어. 🔊 | |
| 19 | 나 벌써 그 애한테 물어봤어.<br>완전히 준비되지 않았대. 🔊 | [완전히 ~하지 않은 (2% 부족한) not quite] |
| 20 | 그 애가 사람 많다고 했어.<br>난 가고 싶은지 모르겠어. 🔊 | |

# Speaking Practice 1min

## 긍정문

☞ 오른쪽 힌트를 이용해서, 직접 문장을 만들어보세요!

| | | |
|---|---|---|
| 21 | 그 애가 나 어려 보인대. | |
| 22 | 너 이거 필요하다며, 그래서 (내가 널 위해) 이거 샀어. | |
| 23 | 그 애가 좋다고 했어. (그거 좋아한다고)<br>그 애 웃는 거 봐서 기분 좋았어. | |
| 24 | Jim이 알고 있다고 나한테 말했어.<br>난 그 애가 알고 있는 줄 몰랐어. | |
| 25 | 너 그거 있다며.<br>그건 어떻게 됐어? (그거한테 무슨 일이 생겼어?) 잃어버렸니? | |
| 26 | 너 그거 안 좋다며.<br>뭐가 네 마음을 바꾼 거야? | |
| 27 | 난 아무것도 후회하지 않는다고 했어. | |
| 28 | 너 그거에 대해서는 아무것도 모른다며.<br>그래서 너한테 물어보지 않은 건데. | [그래서~다, 그게~한 이유다<br>That's why] |
| 29 | Ted는 시간 없대.<br>도와주지 못한다고 했어. | |
| 30 | 그 애가 기억이 안 난다 하더라고.<br>더 이상 물어보고 싶지 않았어. | |

# Speaking Practice
**1min**

## 긍정문

☞ 오른쪽 힌트를 이용해서, 직접 문장을 만들어보세요!

| | | |
|---|---|---|
| 31 | 그 애가 우리 여기 2시까지 와야 된다 했는데. 모두 어디 있지? | |
| 32 | 내 친구가 넌 이거 고칠 수 있다던데. | |
| 33 | 네가 나랑 거기 가고 싶다고 했잖아. | |
| 34 | 어젯밤에 전화한다며. 네 전화 기다렸어. | |
| 35 | 그 애는 일하고 있대. 나한테 바쁘다고 했어. | |
| 36 | 그 애가 너를 만나보고 싶대. | |
| 37 | 내가 너 도와줄 수 있다고 했잖아. 왜 내 도움 안 받으려고 해? (왜 내가 도와주도록 허락하지 않아?) | [도와주게 허락하다 let-help] |
| 38 | 내가 그거 나중에 한다고 했잖아. 그냥 둬. | |
| 39 | 나 그 애한테 어디 가야 한다고 말하고 나왔어. | [나오다, 나가다 leave] |
| 40 | 그 애가 그거 찾으러 올 거라고 했어. | |

Unit 8

# Speaking Practice 1min

## 긍정문

☞ 오른쪽 힌트를 이용해서, 직접 문장을 만들어보세요!

| | | |
|---|---|---|
| 41 | 그 애가 나보고 너한테 물어보라고 했어.<br>너는 알 거라고. | |
| 42 | Bill이 그러던데 네가 여기서 날 기다리고 있다고.<br>무슨 일이야? | [무슨 일이야? What's up?] |
| 43 | 그 애가 나 환불받을 수 있다고 했는데. | [환불받다 get a refund] |
| 44 | 내가 너한테 모든 게 잘 될 거라고 말했잖아. | [(일) 잘되다 work out] |
| 45 | 너 이거 하고 싶다고 했지? (그렇지) | |
| 46 | 그 애가 한 3시간 걸릴 거라고 했어.<br>그리고 돈은 별로 안 들 거래. | [별로 much] |
| 47 | 너 일해야 된다며.<br>지금 회사에 있어야 되는 거 아니야? | [~해야 돼, 하기로 되어있다 be supposed to] |
| 48 | 그 애가 모든 게 잘 진행되고 있다고 했어. | [잘 (진행) 되다 go well] |
| 49 | 네가 나 이해한다며.<br>그것도 거짓말이었니? | [거짓말 a lie] |
| 50 | 누군가가 이 쿠폰 여기서 쓸 수 있다고 했는데요.<br>이거 쓸 수 있나요? | |

# Speaking Practice
## 1min

## 긍정문

☞ 오른쪽 힌트를 이용해서, 직접 문장을 만들어보세요!

| | | |
|---|---|---|
| 51 | 그 애가 금방 우리한테 알려준다고 했어. | |
| 52 | 너 나랑 같이 갈 수 있다며. | |
| 53 | Jenny는 친구랑 공부하고 있대.<br>늦을 거라고 했어. | |
| 54 | 그 애가 그러는데 우리 그거 인터넷으로 할 수 있대.<br>내가 왜 전에 그 생각을 못 했었지? | |
| 55 | 네가 나 그거 오늘 받을 거라고 했잖아. | |
| 56 | Gary가 시간 충분히 있을 거라고 나한테 말했어. | |
| 57 | 내가 그 애한테 혼자 있게 해달라고 했어.<br>내가 혼자 있고 싶다고 했어. | [혼자 내버려/있게 두다<br>leave-alone] |
| 58 | 그 애가 볼일 좀 봐야 된다고 나한테 말했어. | [볼일 보다/있다<br>run (some) errands] |
| 59 | 내가 그 애한테 그거 하지 말라고 했는데.<br>시간 낭비하고 있는 거라고 했어. | |
| 60 | 내가 그 애 사랑한다고 말했어.<br>너무 일렀나? | [너무 이른 too soon] |

# Speaking Practice 1min

## 긍정문

☞ 오른쪽 힌트를 이용해서, 직접 문장을 만들어보세요!

| 61 | Tom은 못 온대. | |
|---|---|---|
| 62 | 나 그거 안 해도 된다며. | |
| 63 | 그 애가 문제없을 거라고 나한테 확실히 말했는데. 이상하네. | [확실히 말하다, 장담하다 assure 이상한 odd] |
| 64 | 내가 너한테 그거 하기 싫다고 했잖아. | |
| 65 | 내가 너는 그거 더 이상 걱정 안 해도 된다고 했잖아. 날 믿어. | |
| 66 | 그 애는 아무것도 안 하고 있다고 했어. 시간 있대. | [시간 있는 free] |
| 67 | 너 그거 다시는 안 할 거라며. 약속했잖아. | |
| 68 | 그 애가 그러는데, 나 이거 취소 못한대. | |
| 69 | 그 애는 안 온다고 했는데. | |
| 70 | 그 애는 더 이상 날 보고 싶지 않다고 했어. | |

# Speaking Practice 1min

## 긍정문

☞ 오른쪽 힌트를 이용해서, 직접 문장을 만들어보세요.

| 71 | 그 애가 열쇠를 잃어버렸대. | |
|---|---|---|
| 72 | 난 그 애한테 까먹었다고 말했어.<br>난 그에게 진실을 말했어. | [진실을 말하다<br>tell-the truth] |
| 73 | 그 애 일 끝나서 오는 길이래. | |
| 74 | 그 애는 그거 안 지 좀 됐다고 나한테 말했어. | [좀 (오래) for a while] |
| 75 | 그 애는 그 영화 이미 봤대. | |
| 76 | 나 그거 안 했다고 너한테 말했잖아. | |
| 77 | Mark는 그 애한테 아무 말도 안 했다고 했어.<br>그 애가 그한테 말한 거 같지 않아. | |
| 78 | 그 애는 그날 너 못 봤다던데. (본 적 없다 했어) | |
| 79 | 그 애가 (그거) 쉽지 않았다고 나한테 말했어.<br>그 애는 힘든 시간을 보내고 있었다더라고. | [힘든 시간 보내다<br>go through a hard time] |
| 80 | 너 이거 전에 안 해봤다며. | |

Unit 8

181

# Speaking Practice 1min

## 부정문

☞ 오른쪽 힌트를 이용해서, 직접 문장을 만들어보세요!

| | | |
|---|---|---|
| 81 | 난 이거 하고 싶다고 하지 않았어. | |
| 82 | 난 (그게) 급하다고 하지 않았어. | |
| 83 | 난 그게 유일한 방법이라고 하지 않았어.<br>이걸 하는 다른 방법들도 있어. | [유일한 방법 the only way<br>다른 방법 other ways] |
| 84 | 난 그게 나쁘다고 하지 않았어.<br>좋지도 나쁘지도 않아. | [좋지도 나쁘지도 않은<br>neither good nor bad] |
| 85 | 그 애가 이거 힘들 거라고 하지 않았는데. | |
| 86 | 너 그거 해봤다고 하지 않았어. | |
| 87 | 그 앤 그게 너의 잘못이라고 말하지 않았어.<br>네가 오해한 거 같아. | [오해하다 misunderstand] |
| 88 | 난 그게 불가능하다고 하지 않았어. | |
| 89 | 난 그걸 할 거라고 하지 않았어.<br>생각 중이라고 했지. | |
| 90 | 아무도 내가 이걸 할 수 있다고 하지 않았어.<br>하지만 난 이걸 할 수 있을 줄 알았어. 난 나 자신을 믿었어. | [믿다 believe in] |

## Speaking Practice 1min

## 의문문

☞ 오른쪽 힌트를 이용해서, 직접 문장을 만들어보세요!

| | | |
|---|---|---|
| 91 | 그게 오늘이라고 했었니?<br>몇 시라고 했지? | |
| 92 | 그 애가 너 이거 필요할 거라고 했어? | |
| 93 | 너 내가 거기에 몇 시까지 가야 된다고 했었지? | |
| 94 | 너 언제 전화한다고? | |
| 95 | 너 그 애를 언제 만난다고? | |
| 96 | 너 어느 거 가지고 싶다고 했었지? | |
| 97 | 내가 미안하다고 했었나? | |
| 98 | 너 어디 간다고 했지? | |
| 99 | 너 올 수 있다고 하지 않았어? | |
| 100 | 너 이거 원한다고 하지 않았어? | |

Unit 8

# Review

복습 강의 바로 듣기

| Positive (긍정) | | Negative (부정) | Question |
|---|---|---|---|
| So do I. | | Neither do I. | - |
| 나도 | | | - |
| Do you? | | Don't you? | - |
| 그래? 정말? | | | - |
| - | | - | Who 동사? What 동사? |
| - | | - | 누가? 뭐가? |
| - | | - | Don't you? |
| - | | - | 안 해? |
| I had p.p. | | I hadn't p.p. | Had you p.p.? |
| 했어, 했었어 (그전에) | | 안 했어, 안 했었어 | 했어? 했었어? |
| I had been -ing | | I hadn't been -ing | Had you been -ing? |
| 했었어 (계속) 하고 있었어 | | 안 했었어 안 하고 있었어 | 했었어? 하고 있었어? |
| I want you to | | I don't want you to | Do you want me to? |
| 하면 좋겠어, 하길 바라 | | 안 하면 좋겠어 | 할까? 하면 좋겠어? |
| I told you to | I told you not to | I didn't tell you to | Did you tell me to? |
| 하래 하라고 했어 | 하지 말래 하지 말라고 했어 | 하라고 안 했어 | 하라고 했어? |
| He said (that) | | He didn't say | Did he say? |
| 했대, 했다고 했어 | | 했다고 안 했어 | 했다고 했어? |

## break & a breakthrough

배운 내용을 생각하며, 직접 문장을 만들어보세요!

정답확인 : P 275

| 01 | 조심해! 그거 깨질 수도 있어. |
|---|---|
| 02 | 그거 정말 약해. 쉽게 깨져. [약한, 손상되기 쉬운 fragile] |
| 03 | 우리 헤어졌어. [헤어지다 break up (with)] |
| 04 | 그거 또 고장 날 수 있어. [고장 나다 break down] |
| 05 | 아무것도 그를 부술 순 없어. 그는 정말 강해. |
| 06 | 그 말 그만해. 가슴 아파. (네가 내 가슴을 아프게 해) [가슴 아프게 하다 break one's heart] |
| 07 | 가슴 아팠어. (그게 날 가슴 아프게 했어) <br> -그랬어? |
| 08 | 그 애한테 말하지 마. 그 애 가슴 아플 거야. (그러면 그게 그의 가슴을 아프게 할 거야) |
| 09 | 그 애가 그거 고장 났대. |
| 10 | 내가 그거 깨지 말라고 했잖아. |
| 11 | 그거 예전엔 맨날 고장 났었어. [맨날, 아주 자주 all the time] |
| 12 | 너의 이런 모습을 보는 거 가슴 아프다. (너 이런 거 보는 거 내 가슴을 아프게 해) |
| 13 | (난 네가) 이거 깨지 않았으면 좋겠어. |
| 14 | 그거 내가 안 깼어. 나 아니야. (그건 내가 아니었어) |
| 15 | 그거 안 깨져. (그거 안 깨질걸) 그건 깨는 게 불가능해. |

Unit 8

# Review

| | |
|---|---|
| 16 | 그 앤 약속 안 어겨. 절대. [약속 깨다/어기다 break promises] |
| 17 | 넌 한 번도 (절대) 약속을 깬 적이 없어. |
| 18 | (난) 내 약속을 깰 수가 없었어. |
| 19 | 그 애한테 한 약속을 깨고 싶지 않아. |
| 20 | (나) 법 어기는 거 아니야. (난 법을 위반하고 있지 않아) [법 어기다/위반하다 break the law] |
| 21 | (우리) 법 어기면 안 돼. 그리고 너도. |
| 22 | 난 법 위반하고 있던 거 아니야. |
| 23 | 그게 어떻게 깨졌는지 모르겠어. |
| 24 | 난 그 애의 가슴을 아프게 하지 않을 거야. 난 그렇게 못해. |
| 25 | 내 가슴 아프게 하지 마. |
| 26 | 나랑 헤어지자는 거야? (너 지금 나랑 헤어지는 거야?) |
| 27 | 너 그 애랑 왜 헤어졌어? |
| 28 | 그 애랑 헤어지지 않았어? |
| 29 | 그 애랑 헤어지고 싶어? |
| 30 | 이거 누가 깼어? 네가 깼어? |

## break & a breakthrough

배운 내용을 생각하며, 직접 문장을 만들어보세요!

| 31 | 그거 또 고장 났어? |
|---|---|
| 32 | 너 이거 깨려고 그랬어? |
| 33 | 이거 깨질 거 같아? |
| 34 | 내가 이거 깰까? |
| 35 | 이거 누가 깼는지 알아? |
| 36 | 넌 왜 약속을 지키지 않아? (왜 약속을 어겨?) |
| 37 | 너 잔 몇 개 깼어? (지금까지) |
| 38 | 우리는 돌파구가 필요해. [돌파구, 중요한 진전 a breakthrough] |
| 39 | 이건 돌파구야! |
| 40 | 여러분, (큰 획을 긋는) **전환점인 순간입니다.** (돌파구적인 순간입니다) **축하합시다.** [축하/기념하다 celebrate] |
| 41 | 그건 과학계에서 엄청난 돌파구였어. [엄청난, 거대한 huge] |
| 42 | 그건 내가 기다려온 돌파구일지도 몰라. |

Unit 8

187

# Dialogue Practice

**Reported Speech**

**A**: Are we going somewhere?

**B**: Yes, we are going to Jenny's birthday party.
I told you about it last week. You said you could go.
Don't you remember?

**A**: Sorry, I totally forgot about that.

**B**: How could you forget? You said it was perfect,
because we hadn't seen her for a while.
And you said you had wanted to meet her boyfriend.

**A**: Yeah, I remember now. I didn't know it was today.

**B**: We should leave soon. Jenny told us to be on time.
She told us not to be late.

**A**: Okay, I promised you I could go, so I will go.

**B**: She sent me the link to the restaurant.
I'm looking at it now.
She said it was a great place for a birthday party.

**A**: I'm ready, let's go. Did she say she had been there?

**B**: Yes, she did. She said it was a foodie spot.

**A**: Oh, that's good.

# Dialogue Practice

**Reported Speech**

A: 우리 어디 가? (우리 지금 어딘가 가?)

B: 어, (우리) Jenny (의) 생일 파티 가잖아.
내가 지난주에 (이거에 대해서) 너한테 말했잖아.
갈 수 있다며. 기억 안 나?

A: 미안, 완전히 (그거에 대해) 까먹고 있었네.

B: 어떻게 잊을 수가 있어?
(너) 그게 완벽하다고 했잖아, 우리가 그 애를 안 본 지 좀 돼서.
그리고 그 애 남자친구 만나고 싶다고도 했잖아.

A: 어, 이제 기억나.
(난 그게) 오늘인 줄 몰랐어.

B: 우리 곧 나가야지. (나가는 게 좋겠다)
Jenny가 제시간에 오라고 했어. 늦지 말라고 (했어).
[제시간에 on time]

---

○ ○ ○ ○ ○ ○ ○

**어떻게 잊을 수가 있어?**

└ How could you forget?
└ How can you forget?

둘 다 좋아요!
Could 사용하는 문장이 조금 더
강렬한 느낌이에요!

**A**: 알았어, 내가 갈 수 있다고 (너한테) 약속했으니, 갈게.

**B**: 그 애가 (Jenny) 식당 링크 보냈어.
(나) 지금 그거 보고 있어. [링크 the link to]
생일 파티하기에 (생일파티 위해) 좋은 곳이래.

**A**: 다 됐어 (난 준비되었어), 가자. 그 애도 거기 가봤대?

**B**: 응. 맛집이래. [맛집 a foodie spot]

**A**: 오, 잘 됐다. (좋다)

# Unit

# 9

누군가 물어봤던 말을
전달하고 싶을 때

## Unit 9

### 누군가 물어봤던 말을 전달하고 싶을 때

# I asked you "했냐고 물어봤어"

간접화법 세 번째 파트는, 누군가 물어봤던 말을 전달하는 경우예요. 의문의 문장을 전달할 때 역시도, 이미 했던 질문의 전달이라서 그 문장의 과거형으로 연결해요. 하지만, 질문의 문장 그대로 하면 긍정문에 의문을 넣는 경우가 되어서, 다시 **평서문으로** 바꾸어 줘야 해요!

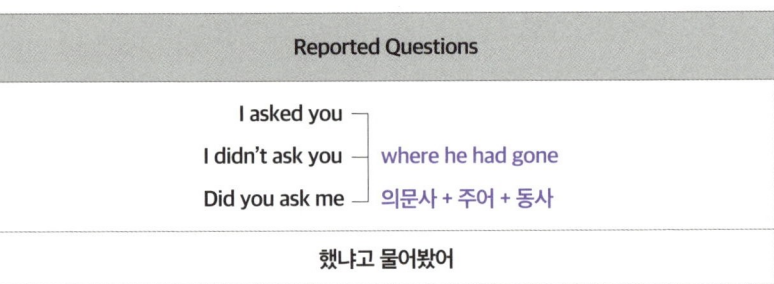

뒤에 연결하는 문장의 경우, 간접 의문 파트 (3권 6~7단원) 와 동일하게 가요. 긍정이나 부정, 혹은 의문에 의문을 넣지 않고, **의문사 뒤에 주어 동사** 순으로 말합니다!

I asked you **의문사 + 주어 + 동사**

거기에, 간접화법이라서 **과거의 문장으로 시제 변환**도 일어나요!

| 직접화법 | 간접화법 |
|---|---|
| "**What are you** doing?" | I asked you **what you were** doing. |
| "**Where have you** been?" | He asked me **where I had** been. |

**<주의: if/whether>**

간접 의문 파트 에서와 동일하게, 의문사가 없는 문장의 경우에는 if 나 whether 를 넣어야 돼요!

| 직접화법 | 간접화법 |
|---|---|
| "**Can you** do it?" | He asked me **if I could** do it. |

## 긍정문

☞ 오른쪽 힌트를 이용해서, 직접 문장을 만들어보세요!

정답확인 : P 276

| 01 | 내가 그 사람한테 그게 얼마인지 물어봤어.<br>45,000원이래. | |
|----|----|----|
| 02 | 그 애가 나한테 그게 어디 있는지 물어봤어.<br>모른다고 했어. | |
| 03 | 내가 너한테 그게 어떠냐고 물었었잖아.<br>그리고 넌 그게 재밌다며. | |
| 04 | 그 애가 나한테 네가 어디 있는지 물었고,<br>난 그에게 회사에 있다고 말했어. | |
| 05 | 내가 그 애한테 몇 살인지 물어봤어.<br>29살이래. | |
| 06 | 내가 그 애한테 그게 언제인지 물었는데,<br>다음 주 월요일이랬어. | |
| 07 | 그 애가 나한테 이게 뭐냐고 물었고,<br>난 대답을 못했어. | |
| 08 | 내가 그 애한테 그게 얼마일지 물었고,<br>그는 비싸지 않을 거라고 했어. | |
| 09 | 그 애가 나한테 네 이름 (이 뭐냐고) 물었어. | |
| 10 | 내가 그 애한테 뭘 걱정하냐고 물었었어. | |

## Speaking Practice — 1min

긍정문

☞ 오른쪽 힌트를 이용해서, 직접 문장을 만들어보세요!

| 11 | 그 애가 나한테 이게 이런지 얼마나 된 건지 물었어.<br>뭐라고 말할지 모르겠더라. | [이런지 like this] |
|---|---|---|
| 12 | 그 애가 나한테 내 계획이 뭔지 물었어.<br>계획이 없어서 난 아무 말 못 했어. | |
| 13 | 그가 나한테 내 종교가 뭔지 물었어. | |
| 14 | 난 그 애한테 어떻게 지냈는지 물어봤어.<br>잘 지냈대. | |
| 15 | 난 그 애한테 그게 언제 될지 물어봤어.<br>그는 나한테 한 시간이면 될 거라고 했어. | [(다) 된, 준비된 ready] |
| 16 | 그 애가 나한테 어느 나라 사람인지 물었어. (어디 출신인지)<br>난 한국 사람이라고 그에게 말했어. | |
| 17 | 내가 그 애한테 언제 돌아올 건지 물었어.<br>모른대. | |
| 18 | 난 나 자신에게 내가 왜 그렇게 화가 난 건지 물었어.<br>화날 이유가 없었어. | [그렇게 화난 so angry] |
| 19 | 이게 언제 끝이 날지 너한테 물어보고 싶었어. | [끝나는, 끝인 over] |
| 20 | 내가 그 애한테 가장 좋아하는 색이 뭐냐고 물어봤어.<br>노란색이래. | |

# Speaking Practice
## 1min

## 긍정문

☞ 오른쪽 힌트를 이용해서, 직접 문장을 만들어보세요!

| | | |
|---|---|---|
| 21 | 내가 그 애한테 난 뭐가 필요한지 물었어. | |
| 22 | 그 애가 뭘 하고 있는지 물어봤어.<br>일하고 있대. | |
| 23 | 내가 그 애한테 거기 가는 데 얼마나 걸릴지 물어봤어.<br>2시간 걸릴 거래. | |
| 24 | 그 애가 나한테 그거 바꾸려면 얼마 드는지 물어보던데. | |
| 25 | 그 애가 나 어디 갔다 왔는지 물어보더라. | |
| 26 | 내가 그 애한테 어떻게 그렇게 성공했는지 물어봤어. | [성공하다]<br>become (so) successful |
| 27 | 내가 그 애한테 무슨 말이 하고 싶은지 물었어.<br>하고 싶은 말이 아무것도 없대. | |
| 28 | 그 애는 내가 뭘 좋아하는지, 주말엔 뭘 하는지 물었어.<br>내게 많은 질문을 했어. | |
| 29 | 그 애가 나한테 내가 언제 왔는지 물었어.<br>내가 어떻게 여기 왔는지도 물었어. | [~도, 또한 also] |
| 30 | 난 그 애한테 어디서 그걸 샀는지 물어봤어.<br>기억 안 난대. (기억 못한다고 말했어) | |

## Speaking Practice
### 1min

## 긍정문

☞ 오른쪽 힌트를 이용해서, 직접 문장을 만들어보세요!

| | | |
|---|---|---|
| 31 | 내가 너한테 내일 뭐 할 건지 물었잖아. | |
| 32 | 그 애가 나한테 얼마나 오래 기다렸는지 물었어. | |
| 33 | 그 애가 나한테 어디 있을 거냐고 물어봐서, 여기에 있을 거라고 그에게 말했어. | |
| 34 | 난 네가 왜 그걸 해야만 했냐고 물었잖아. 넌 내 질문에 완전히 대답하지 않았고. | [완전히 ~하지 않은 (2% 부족한) not quite] |
| 35 | 그 애가 나한테 뭐 입을 건지 물어봤어. | |
| 36 | 그 애가 나한테 무슨 일이 일어났냐고 물어보면 어떡해? 난 뭐라고 말해? | [(만일)~하면 (어떡하지?) What if?] |
| 37 | 그 애가 나한테 왜 차단했냐고 물어보면 어떡하지? 난 뭐라고 말할까? | [차단하다 block] |
| 38 | 그 애가 너한테 너 어디 있었냐고 물어보면? 거짓말할 거야? | |
| 39 | 그 애가 너한테 왜 그거 아직 안 했냐고 물어보면 어떡 할 거야? | |
| 40 | 그 애가 나한테 왜 네가 안 왔냐고 물어보면? | |

Unit 9

## 긍정문

☞ 오른쪽 힌트를 이용해서, 직접 문장을 만들어보세요!

| 41 | 내가 그 애한테 그거 언제 할 건지 물어봤어.<br>이번 주말에 할 거래. | |
|---|---|---|
| 42 | 내가 그 애한테 어느 거 사야 되는지 물어봤어. | |
| 43 | 그 애가 나한테 어디 가냐고 물어봤어.<br>근데 난 대답하고 싶지 않았어. | |
| 44 | 그 애가 나한테 너 언제 올 수 있냐고 물었어. | |
| 45 | 그 애가 나한테 너 어디 사냐고 물었어.<br>그 애한테 말 안 했어. | |
| 46 | 그 애가 나한테 뭐 봤는지 물었어.<br>아무것도 안 봤다고 말했어. | |
| 47 | 그가 내게 우리가 서로 안 지 얼마나 오래되었는지 물어봤어. | |
| 48 | 난 너한테 너라면 어떻게 할지 (뭘 할지) 물어보고 싶었어, 입장이 바뀌었다면 말이야. | [입장/지위/역할 바뀌었다면<br>if the roles were reversed] |
| 49 | 네 생일에 뭐 갖고 싶은지 물어보고 싶었어. | |
| 50 | 그 애가 왜 그걸 못하는지 물어보고 싶지만, 못 물어봤어. | |

## Speaking Practice 1min

### 긍정문

☞ 오른쪽 힌트를 이용해서, 직접 문장을 만들어보세요!

| | | |
|---|---|---|
| 51 | 그 애가 나한테 내일 우리가 몇 시에 올지 물어봤고, 난 2시에 갈 거라고 했어. 🔊 | |
| 52 | 그 애가 나한테 네가 뭘 좋아하는지 물어보더라. 그 애가 너를 좋아하는 거 같아. 🔊 | |
| 53 | 내가 그 애한테 이거 어떻게 만드는지 물어봤어. 🔊 | |
| 54 | 내가 너한테 뭐 하고 있냐고 물었잖아. 🔊 | |
| 55 | 내가 그 애한테 어디서 일하는지 물어봤는데, 대답하지 않았어. 🔊 | |
| 56 | 난 그 애한테 내가 그를 위해서 뭘 할 수 있는지 물어봤는데, 내가 할 수 있는 것은 아무것도 없대. 🔊 | |
| 57 | 그 애가 나한테 내가 그걸 어떻게 했는지 (그걸로 뭘 했는지) 물어봤어. 뭐라고 말할지 모르겠더라. 🔊 | [~로, ~를 가지고 with] |
| 58 | 내가 그 애한테 얼마 내야 되는지 물어봤는데, 우리 돈 안 내도 된대. 🔊 | |
| 59 | 난 그 애한테 어디에 갈 건지, 누구랑 갈 건지, 그리고 언제 돌아올 건지 물어봤어. 🔊 | |
| 60 | 그는 내게 내가 어디 가고 싶은지, 뭘 하고 싶은지, 어디서 머무르고 싶은지, 얼마나 오래 있을 수 있는지 물었어. 🔊 | |

## Speaking Practice 1min

### if/whether

☞ 오른쪽 힌트를 이용해서, 직접 문장을 만들어보세요!

| 61 | 난 그에게 이게 너무 크냐고 물어봤고,<br>그 애는 괜찮다고 했어. | |
| --- | --- | --- |
| 62 | 난 그 애한테 누군가 이거 쓰고 있냐고 물어봤어.<br>아무도 안 쓴다던데. | |
| 63 | 내가 그 애한테 그거 고칠 수 있냐고 물어봤어.<br>못 고친대. | |
| 64 | 내가 그 애한테 이거 전에 해봤냐고 물어봤어.<br>그리고 그 애는 안 해봤다고 했어. | |
| 65 | 내가 그 애한테 이거 좋아하는지 물어봤어.<br>그렇대. | |
| 66 | 내가 너한테 이거 하고 싶은지 물어봤잖아.<br>넌 그렇다고 했고. | |
| 67 | 난 그에게 시간이 충분히 있는지 물어봤고,<br>그 애는 그렇다고 했어. | |
| 68 | 그 애가 나한테 생각해 볼 수 있겠냐고 물어봤고,<br>난 생각해 보겠다고 했어. | |
| 69 | 난 그에게 내가 그걸 해도 되는지 물어봤고,<br>그 앤 그렇다고 했어. | |
| 70 | 난 그 애한테 그게 진심이냐고 물어봤어.<br>진심이랬어. | [진심이다 mean] |

## Speaking Practice 1min

### if/whether

☞ 오른쪽 힌트를 이용해서, 직접 문장을 만들어보세요!

| | | |
|---|---|---|
| 71 | 내가 너한테 거기 가봤냐고 물어봤잖아.<br>너 거기 안 가봤다고 하지 않았어? | |
| 72 | 그 애가 나한테 네가 올 수 있는지 물어봤어. | |
| 73 | 그 애가 나한테 내일 오냐고 물었어.<br>난 생각 중이라고 그 애한테 말했어. | |
| 74 | 그 애가 나한테 내가 그를 이해해 줄 수 있는지 물어봤어.<br>난 그를 이해할 수 있는지 모르겠어. | |
| 75 | 내가 그 애한테 날 사랑하는지 물어봤어. | |
| 76 | 그 애는 내가 일본 사람이냐고 물었어. | |
| 77 | 그 애는 내가 그걸 썼는지 (사용) 물어봤어. | |
| 78 | 그 애가 나한테 우리가 오래 기다렸는지 물어봤어. | |
| 79 | 내가 너한테 그거 원하는지 물어봤었잖아.<br>네가 필요 없다며. | |
| 80 | 내가 그 애한테 널 아는지 물어봤어.<br>안다고 하던데. | |

Unit 9                                                               203

## 부정문

☞ 오른쪽 힌트를 이용해서, 직접 문장을 만들어보세요!

| | | |
|---|---|---|
| 81 | 넌 나한테 내가 뭐가 필요한지 물어보지 않았잖아.<br>한 번도 안 물어봐. (넌 절대 안 해) | [한 번도, 절대 ~안 해 never] |
| 82 | 그 애가 나한테 올 수 있냐고 물어보지 않았어.<br>날 초대하지 않았어. | |
| 83 | 난 그 애의 생각이 뭔지 물어본 게 아니야.<br>난 너한테 네가 어떻게 생각하는지 물어봤어.<br>네가 뭘 하고 싶은지 말해줘. | |
| 84 | 넌 나한테 내 기분이 어떤지도 물어보지 않았어.<br>내가 어떤 기분인지 알고 싶지 않아? | [(조차)도 even] |
| 85 | 난 그에게 날 용서해 줄 수 있는지 물어보지 못했어. | |
| 86 | 난 그 애가 왜 그걸 하고 싶어 하는지 묻지 않았어.<br>왜 나는 그 간단한 질문을 하는 걸 생각하지 않았을까? | |
| 87 | 내가 괜찮은지 묻지 말아 줘.<br>지금 당장은 어떻게 대답할지 모르겠어. | |
| 88 | 그는 나한테 내 하루가 어떤지 묻지 않았어.<br>나도 그랬고. 우린 대화를 멈추었어. | [대화/소통하다 communicate] |
| 89 | (나) 그 애한테 돈 얼마 버는지 물어보면 안 되지? | [돈 얼마 how much money<br>벌다 make] |
| 90 | 사람들한테 나이랑 직업을 물어보면 안 돼.<br>(우린 그들이 몇 살인지, 뭐 하는지 안 묻는 게 좋겠어)<br>실례가 될 수 있어, 그들을 처음 만날 때면. | [실례인, 예의 없는 impolite<br>처음 for the first time] |

## Speaking Practice 1min

## 의문문

☞ 오른쪽 힌트를 이용해서, 직접 문장을 만들어보세요!

| 91 | 그 애한테 뭐 갖고 싶은지 물어봤어? | |
|---|---|---|
| 92 | 그 애 언제 올 건지 물어봤어? | |
| 93 | 그 애가 어디에 있는지 물어봤어? | |
| 94 | 그 애가 왜 그러는지 (그걸 하는지) 물어봤어? | |
| 95 | 우리가 뭘 해야 되는지 그 애한테 물어봤어? | |
| 96 | 우리 여기 있어도 되는지 그 애한테 물어봤어? | |
| 97 | 그게 괜찮은지 물어봤어? | |
| 98 | 그게 언제일지 물어봤어? | |
| 99 | 내가 너 어떤지 물어봤었나? | |
| 100 | 우리가 그 애한테 우릴 도와줄 수 있는지 안 물어봤었나? | |

Unit 9

# Review

복습 강의 바로 듣기

| Positive (긍정) | | Negative (부정) | Question |
|---|---|---|---|
| So do I. | | Neither do I. | - |
| 나도 | | | - |
| Do you? | | Don't you? | - |
| 그래? 정말? | | | - |
| - | | - | Who 동사? What 동사? |
| - | | - | 누가? 뭐가? |
| - | | - | Don't you? |
| - | | - | 안 해? |
| I had p.p. | | I hadn't p.p. | Had you p.p.? |
| 했어, 했었어 (그전에) | | 안 했어, 안 했었어 | 했어? 했었어? |
| I had been -ing | | I hadn't been -ing | Had you been -ing? |
| 했었어 (계속) 하고 있었어 | | 안 했었어 안 하고 있었어 | 했었어? 하고 있었어? |
| I want you to | | I don't want you to | Do you want me to? |
| 하면 좋겠어, 하길 바라 | | 안 하면 좋겠어 | 할까? 하면 좋겠어? |
| I told you to | I told you not to | I didn't tell you to | Did you tell me to? |
| 하래 하라고 했어 | 하지 말래 하지 말라고 했어 | 하라고 안 했어 | 하라고 했어? |
| He said (that) | | He didn't say | Did he say? |
| 했대, 했다고 했어 | | 했다고 안 했어 | 했다고 했어? |
| I asked you | | I didn't ask you | Did you ask me? |
| 했냐고 물어봤어 | | 했냐고 묻지 않았어 | 했냐고 물어봤어? |

206  기초영어 1000문장 말하기 연습 4

## meet & meet sb halfway

배운 내용을 생각하며, 직접 문장을 만들어보세요!

정답확인 : P 279

| 01 | 그를 만나보고 싶어. |
| --- | --- |
| 02 | (너) 거기서 누구 만날지도 모르잖아. (누군가 만날 수도 있어) |
| 03 | 그 애를 만나봐. (만나보는 게 좋겠어) 넌 그 애를 좋아할 거야. |
| 04 | (난 널) 내일 만날 수 있어. |
| 05 | 그래, 거기서 만나자. (거기서 널 만날게) |
| 06 | 나 그 애 만나본 적 있어. (전에 만나봤어) |
| 07 | 우리 여기서 만난 지 오래됐어. |
| 08 | 네가 그 애 만나봤으면 좋겠어. |
| 09 | 나 학교 끝나고 친구 만나려고 했는데.<br>-그랬어? |
| 10 | 우리 예전엔 매일 만났었어. |
| 11 | 난 새로운 사람들을 만나는 게 좋아. |
| 12 | 널 만나서 정말 반가웠어. |
| 13 | (너) 내 가족들과 금방 만나게 될 거야. |
| 14 | 우리 2010년에 처음 만났어. |
| 15 | 우린 목요일마다 만나. |

# Review

| | |
|---|---|
| 16 | 널 만나는 걸 기대해. [기대/고대하다 look forward to -ing] |
| 17 | 마음이 맞는 사람을 만나는 게 어려워.<br>[비슷한 마인드를 가진 사람, 마음 맞는 사람 like-minded people] |
| 18 | (네가 날) 오늘 만날 수 있다며. |
| 19 | 우리 더 이상 만나지 않는 게 좋을 것 같아. |
| 20 | 나 그 애와 다시는 안 만날 거야. |
| 21 | 나 그 애와 다시는 만나고 싶지 않아. |
| 22 | 이번 주에는 널 못 만나. |
| 23 | 우리 만난 적 없어. |
| 24 | 그 앤 새로운 사람을 안 만나. 내향인이야. [내향인 an introvert] |
| 25 | 넌 아직 인연을 만나지 않은 거야. [맞는 사람, 인연 the right person] |
| 26 | 나 그 애 안 만났어. 야근해야 된대서. [야근하다, 늦게까지 일하다 work late] |
| 27 | 난 평생 아무도 못 만날 것 같아. [평생 ever] |
| 28 | 난 그를 다시는 안 만날지도 몰라. |
| 29 | 우리 거기서 만나지 못했어. |
| 30 | 너 친구들 만날 거라며. 그 애들 어디서 만날 거야? |

## meet & meet sb halfway

배운 내용을 생각하며, 직접 문장을 만들어보세요!

| | |
|---|---|
| 31 | 내가 그 애를 만나야 돼? |
| 32 | 내가 인연을 언제 만날 거 같아? |
| 33 | 너는 그 애와 만나봤어? |
| 34 | 몇 시에 만날래? |
| 35 | 너희 어디서 만났어? 어떻게 만났어? |
| 36 | (너) 나 이따 만날 수 있어? |
| 37 | 우리 어디서 만나는 게 좋을까? |
| 38 | 우리 전에 만난 적 없었나? |
| 39 | 친구들 안 만나고 싶어? |
| 40 | 좀! 서로 양보하자. (나랑 타협해)<br>[좀! 제발! Come on! 타협하다, 서로 양보하다 meet sb halfway] |
| 41 | 조금 양보할 수 있어? (나랑 타협할 수 있어?) |
| 42 | 내가 조금 양보할게. 150은 어때? |
| 43 | 우리 타협하는 게 어때? |
| 44 | 네가 타협할 수 없다면, 우린 안될 거야. (그건 안될 거야) |

# Dialogue Practice

**Reported Questions**

A: What was that all about?

B: I don't know. He just asked me a bunch of questions.

A: What did he ask you?

B: He asked me where I was from, and how old I was.

A: That's odd. Why would he ask you that?

B: I thought he was being friendly.

A: And what else did he ask you?

B: He asked me how long I had been here, whether I was enjoying the time here, and if I was alone.

**A**: What did you say?

**B**: I told him the truth.
I said I had been here for 5 days, I was with you, and we were having a great time.

**A**: I think he was hitting on you.

**B**: Do you?

**A**: Yes, I do. Didn't you ask him why he was asking so many questions?

**B**: I was going to, but then you showed up, and he left.

# Dialogue Practice

**Reported Questions**

**A:** 뭐야? (그게 다 무엇에 관한 거였어?)

**B:** 몰라. 그가 그냥 내게 이것저것 질문하더라고.
[이것저것 (여러/많은) 질문 a bunch of questions]

**A:** (그가 네게) 뭘 물어봤는데?

**B:** 내가 어느 나라 사람인지, 몇 살인지 묻더라고.

**A:** 이상하네. [이상한 odd]
왜 너한테 그런 걸 묻는 거지? (왜 그걸 물을까?)

**B:** 난 그가 친절하게 구는 거라고 생각했어.
[친절/상냥하게 구는 being friendly]

**A:** 그리고 뭐 또 (다른 거) 물어봤어? [뭐 또, 뭐 더 what else]

**B:** 내가 여기 온 지 얼마나 됐는지, 여기서 시간을 즐기고 있는지, 그리고 내가 혼자인지 물어봤어.

A: 넌 뭐라 그랬어?

B: 사실대로 말했지. (진실을 말했어)
　여기 온 지 5일 됐고, 너랑 같이 있고,
　우리는 좋은 시간을 보내고 있다고 했어.

A: 너한테 작업 걸고 있던 거 같은데.
　[작업 걸다, 꼬시다, 플러팅하다 hit on sb]

B: 그래?

A: 어. 왜 그렇게 많은 질문을 하는지 안 물어봤어?

B: 그러려고 했는데, 그때 네가 나타났고, 그는 갔어(떠났어).
　[오다, 나타나다 show up]

# Unit

# 10

알고 보니 아닌
현재 사실의 반전을 말하고 싶을 때

# Unit 10
## 알고 보니 아닌 현재 사실의 반전을 말하고 싶을 때

# I thought "한 줄 알았어"

간접화법과 동일하게 시제를 뒤로 변화시키는 것은 "think" 나 "know" 같은 단어들과도 정말 잘 어울려요. 과거형에 초점을 맞추면서, 시제를 동일하게 맞추어 주는 과정에서요. 특히, "I thought" 와는, 알고 보니 아닌 현재 사실의 반전을 말할 때 유용하게 사용할 수 있어요.

| Positive | Negative | Question |
|---|---|---|
| I thought | I didn't know | Did you know? |
| 한 줄 알았어<br>(근데 아니네) | 한 줄 몰랐어 | 한 줄 알았어?<br>알고 있었어? |

"I thought" 는 "생각했다" 이므로, 그렇게 알고 있었는데 알고 보니 아닌 게 되어서 반전을 나타냅니다. 알고 보니 아닌 것이라서, 현재 사실이 아니므로 현재형을 사용할 수 없어요! 그래서 과거형 문장과 함께 사용이 됩니다.

**이렇게 만듭니다!**

I thought 뒤에 과거형 문장을 넣어주면 됩니다!

| 긍정 | 부정 | 의문 |
|---|---|---|
| I thought it was easy.<br>그게 쉬운 줄 알았어.<br>(알고 보니 아님) | I didn't know it was easy.<br>그게 쉬운 줄 몰랐어.<br>(정말 몰랐음) | Did you know it was easy?<br>그게 쉬운 줄 알았어?<br>(알고 있었어?) |

<비교>

| **I thought**<br>한 줄 알았어.<br>(알고 보니 아닌 반전) | **I knew**<br>그럴 줄 알았어. 알고 있었어.<br>(알고 있었고, 지금도 그게 사실임) |
|---|---|
| **I thought I could do it.**<br>내가 이거 할 수 있을 줄 알았어.<br>(근데 못해) | **I knew I could do it.**<br>내가 이거 할 수 있을 줄 알고 있었어.<br>(할 수 있음) |
| **I didn't think you were coming.**<br>네가 올 거라고 생각하지 않았어. | **I didn't know you were coming.**<br>네가 오는 줄 몰랐어. |
| **Did you think you had to go?**<br>네가 가야 된다고 생각했어? | **Did you know you had to go?**<br>네가 가야 되는 거 알고 있었어? |

# Speaking Practice — 1min

## 긍정문
☞ 오른쪽 힌트를 이용해서, 직접 문장을 만들어보세요!

정답확인 : P 280

| 01 | 미안, 이거 내 건 줄 알았어. | |
|---|---|---|
| 02 | 난 당신이 다른 사람인 줄 알았어요. | [다른 사람 someone else] |
| 03 | 난 (그게) 오늘인 줄 알았어. 네가 오늘이라고 하지 않았니? | |
| 04 | 난 그게 더 쉬운 줄 알았어. 어려운 줄 몰랐어. (어렵다고 생각하지 않았어) | |
| 05 | 모두 다 그게 쉬울 거라고 생각했어. | |
| 06 | 난 그게 여기 있는 줄 알았어. 이상하네. 내가 그거 여기다 둔 줄 알았어. | [이상한 odd] |
| 07 | 난 너 괜찮은 줄 알았어. 왜 나한테 말 안 했어? | |
| 08 | 난 그 애가 아픈 줄 알았어. 목소리가 안 좋았어. | [목소리 (몸 상태) 좋다 sound well] |
| 09 | 난 그걸 하는 게 불가능할 줄 알았어. | |
| 10 | 난 진짜 그게 비싼 줄 알았어. (진짜 그렇게 생각했어) | |

# Speaking Practice
## 1min

## 긍정문

☞ 오른쪽 힌트를 이용해서, 직접 문장을 만들어보세요!

| | | |
|---|---|---|
| 11 | 난 네가 일하고 있는 줄 알았어.<br>방해하고 싶지 않았어. | [방해하다 bother] |
| 12 | 난 너한테 그거 있는 줄 알았어. | |
| 13 | 우리 모두 네가 알고 있는 줄 알았어. | |
| 14 | 난 그 애를 안다고 생각했었어.<br>한길 사람 속은 모른다더니. | [한 길사람 속은 모른다<br>You think you know someone.] |
| 15 | 난 내가 널 위해서 그거 할 수 있는 줄 알았어. | |
| 16 | 그 애는 내가 이걸 가지고 싶어 한다고 생각했어. | |
| 17 | 난 훨씬 더 오래 걸릴 줄 알았어. | [훨씬 더 오래 much longer] |
| 18 | 그거 하려면 돈 많이 드는 줄 알았어. | |
| 19 | 네가 전화할 줄 알았어. | |
| 20 | 난 네가 올 거라고 생각했어.<br>널 기다리고 있었어. | |

## Speaking Practice (1min)

### 긍정문

☞ 오른쪽 힌트를 이용해서, 직접 문장을 만들어보세요!

| | | |
|---|---|---|
| 21 | 난 다른 사람이 여기 있는 줄 알았어. | [다른 사람 someone else] |
| 22 | 그 애, 이번 주말에 일해야 되는 줄 알았는데. | |
| 23 | 그 애가 우리 도와줄 줄 알았어. | |
| 24 | 난 너 그만 올 줄 알았어. | [그만하다 stop -ing] |
| 25 | 네가 생각해 봤는 줄 알았어. | |
| 26 | 네가 나 거기서 본 줄 알았어. 나 못 봤니? | |
| 27 | 내가 오늘 와야 되는 줄 알았어. | |
| 28 | 네가 거기 가고 싶어 하는 줄 알았어. | |
| 29 | 모두 내가 질 거라고 생각했었어. | |
| 30 | 난 우리가 오늘 만나는 줄 알았어. | |

## 긍정문

☞ 오른쪽 힌트를 이용해서, 직접 문장을 만들어보세요!

| 31 | 나 이거 하고 싶은 줄 알았는데, 아니야. | |
| --- | --- | --- |
| 32 | 네가 여기 전에 와본 줄 알았어. | |
| 33 | 사람이 많을 줄 알았어. | |
| 34 | 난 네가 (그게) 괜찮다고 한 줄 알았어. | |
| 35 | 난 네가 나보고 이거 먼저 하라고 한 줄 알았어. | |
| 36 | 난 네가 이해하는 줄 알았어.<br>네가 내 편인 줄 알았어. | [~편 on one's side] |
| 37 | 우리 모두 그게 될 줄 알았어. | |
| 38 | 네가 자는 줄 알았어.<br>널 깨우고 싶지 않았어. | [깨우다 wake-up] |
| 39 | 비 오는 줄 알았어. | |
| 40 | (그게) 끝난 줄 알았어. | [끝난 over] |

## Speaking Practice 1min

## 긍정문

☞ 오른쪽 힌트를 이용해서, 직접 문장을 만들어보세요!

| 41 | 네가 그거 가져올 줄 알았어. | |
|---|---|---|
| 42 | 난 그 애가 화낼 줄 알았어. | [화나다 get angry] |
| 43 | 난 그 애가 변할 줄 알았어.<br>난 그 애가 변할 수 있다고 믿었어. | |
| 44 | 난 이번엔 (그게) 다를 줄 알았어. | |
| 45 | 우리가 더 많은 시간을 같이 보낼 수 있을 줄 알았는데. | |
| 46 | 난 진짜 그 회사 붙을 줄 알았어.<br>(그 직업 가질 줄 알았어) | [그 회사 붙다 get the job] |
| 47 | 난 내가 그거 한 줄 알았어. | |
| 48 | 너 내가 그거 만든 줄 알았지? | |
| 49 | 난 내가 실수한 줄 알았어. | [실수하다<br>make a mistake] |
| 50 | 난 네가 그 얘기는 안 하고 싶어 할 줄 알았어. | |

# Speaking Practice 1min

## 긍정문

☞ 오른쪽 힌트를 이용해서, 직접 문장을 만들어보세요!

| 51 | 난 네가 모르는 줄 알았지. | |
|---|---|---|
| 52 | 너한테 그거 없는 줄 알았어.<br>그래서 하나 더 가져왔지. | [하나 더, 추가로 extra] |
| 53 | 네가 고기 못 먹는 줄 알았어. | |
| 54 | 네가 오기 싫어하는 줄 알았어.<br>그래서 너한테 안 물어본 거야. | [그래서~다, 그게~한 이유다<br>That's why] |
| 55 | 난 네가 관심 없는 줄 알았지. (신경 안 쓰는 줄) | [신경 쓰다, 관심 있다<br>care] |
| 56 | 난 네가 그 애 보기 싫어하는 줄 알았어. | |
| 57 | 난 네가 이거 안 좋아할 줄 알았어.<br>난 네가 이런 종류의 것들을 좋아하는 줄 몰랐어. | [이런 종류의 것들<br>these kinds of things] |
| 58 | 난 내가 그거 못 바꾸는 줄 알았어. | |
| 59 | 난 그게 상관없는 줄 알았어.<br>그게 중요한 줄 몰랐어. | [상관있다, 중요하다<br>matter] |
| 60 | 난 그 애가 괜찮아할 줄 알았어.<br>(신경 안 쓸 줄 알았어) | [괜찮다, 신경 안 쓴다<br>don't mind (-ing)] |

# Speaking Practice 1min

## I knew

☞ 오른쪽 힌트를 이용해서, 직접 문장을 만들어보세요!

| | | |
|---|---|---|
| 61 | 난 네가 여기 있는 줄 알고 있었어. | |
| 62 | 난 그 애가 올 거라고 알고 있었어. | |
| 63 | 난 네가 이거 좋아할 줄 알고 있었어. | |
| 64 | 난 네가 그거 할 수 있을 줄 알았어. | |
| 65 | 그 애가 나한테 진실을 말하고 있다는 걸 알고 있었어. | [진실을 말하다] tell-the truth] |
| 66 | 난 우리가 결혼하기 전에 그 애가 그런 사람인 줄 알고 있었어. | [그런(사람인) 줄 like that] |
| 67 | 난 내가 그걸 원하는 걸 알았어. 난 그냥 그걸 가져야 했어. | |
| 68 | 우린 네가 이길 줄 알았어. 축하해! | |
| 69 | 난 그 애가 가야 되는 줄(못 있을 줄) 알고 있었어. 나한테 말했어. | |
| 70 | 넌 내가 이거 할 줄 알고 있었지? | |

## Speaking Practice (1min)

**부정문**

☞ 오른쪽 힌트를 이용해서, 직접 문장을 만들어보세요!

| | | |
|---|---|---|
| 71 | 난 네가 여기 있는 줄 몰랐어.<br>언제 왔어? | |
| 72 | 이게 이렇게 작은 줄 몰랐어. | [이렇게 작은 this small] |
| 73 | 내가 이걸 할 수 있는 줄 몰랐어. | |
| 74 | 난 (그게) 이렇게 될 줄 몰랐어. | [(결과/진행) 되다 turn out<br>이렇게 like this] |
| 75 | 난 그 애가 꺼려 할 줄 몰랐어. | [꺼려 하다, 마음에 걸리다 mind] |
| 76 | 네가 그거에 대해 아는 줄 몰랐어. | |
| 77 | 네가 그거 좋아하는 줄 몰랐어. | |
| 78 | 난 내가 그걸 하고 있는 줄도 몰랐어. | [~도, 조차도 even] |
| 79 | 내가 거기 가야 되는 줄 몰랐어.<br>난 네가 우리 보고 오지 말라고 한 줄 알았어. | |
| 80 | 네가 거기 가고 싶어 하는 줄 몰랐어. | |

Unit 10

## Speaking Practice — 1min

### 부정문

☞ 오른쪽 힌트를 이용해서, 직접 문장을 만들어보세요!

| 81 | 너 오는 줄 몰랐어.<br>왜 아무 말 안 했어? | |
|---|---|---|
| 82 | 난 그 애가 그럴 줄 (그거 할 줄) 몰랐어.<br>그런 배짱이 있다고 생각하지 않았어. | [용기/배짱/배포 있다<br>have the courage] |
| 83 | 우린 그거 돈 내야 되는 줄 몰랐어요.<br>공짜인 줄 알았어요. | |
| 84 | 너 올 수 있는 줄 알았지.<br>다른 약속(계획) 있는 줄 몰랐어. | [다른 약속 other plans] |
| 85 | 네가 날 기다리고 있는 줄 몰랐어. | |
| 86 | 문제가 있는 줄 몰랐어요. | |
| 87 | 난 이게 엄청 뜰 (수 있을) 줄 몰랐어.<br>우린 정말 운이 좋았어. | [엄청 뜨다, 조회수 폭발하다<br>go viral ] |
| 88 | 너 거기 가봤는 줄 몰랐어. | |
| 89 | 넌 이런 일이 일어날 줄 몰랐잖아.<br>너의 잘못이 아니야. | |
| 90 | 그게 그렇게 오래갈 줄 아무도 몰랐어. | [오래가다<br>last (that) long] |

## 의문문

☞ 오른쪽 힌트를 이용해서, 직접 문장을 만들어보세요!

| 91 | 내가 여기 있는 줄 어떻게 알았어?<br>누가 너한테 그 말을 했어? | |
| --- | --- | --- |
| 92 | 내가 이거 갖고 싶어 하는 줄 어떻게 알았어? | |
| 93 | 너는 이번 주말에 일해야 되는 거 알고 있었어? | |
| 94 | 내가 전화할 줄 알았어? | |
| 95 | 그 애가 임신한 거 알고 있었어? | [임신한 pregnant] |
| 96 | 네가 모든 걸 다 잃을 수 있다는 걸 알았어? | |
| 97 | 그 애가 성공할 줄 알고 있었어?<br>음, 난 알았지. | [음, 글쎄 well] |
| 98 | 그런 일이 생길 줄 알았어? | |
| 99 | 그게 불법인 거 몰랐어? | [불법인 illegal] |
| 100 | 네가 진짜 안 걸릴 줄 알았어?<br>(안 걸릴 수 있다고 진짜 생각했어?) | [안 걸리다, 안 잡히다, 모면하다 get away with it] |

# Review

| Positive (긍정) | | Negative (부정) | Question |
|---|---|---|---|
| So do I. | | Neither do I. | - |
| 나도 | | | - |
| Do you? | | Don't you? | - |
| 그래? 정말? | | | - |
| - | | - | Who 동사? What 동사? |
| - | | - | 누가? 뭐가? |
| - | | - | Don't you? |
| - | | - | 안 해? |
| I had p.p. | | I hadn't p.p. | Had you p.p.? |
| 했어, 했었어 (그전에) | | 안 했어, 안 했었어 | 했어? 했었어? |
| I had been -ing | | I hadn't been -ing | Had you been -ing? |
| 했었어 (계속) 하고 있었어 | | 안 했었어 안 하고 있었어 | 했었어? 하고 있었어? |
| I want you to | | I don't want you to | Do you want me to? |
| 하면 좋겠어, 하길 바라 | | 안 하면 좋겠어 | 할까? 하면 좋겠어? |
| I told you to | I told you not to | I didn't tell you to | Did you tell me to? |
| 하래 하라고 했어 | 하지 말래 하지 말라고 했어 | 하라고 안 했어 | 하라고 했어? |
| He said (that) | | He didn't say | Did he say? |
| 했대, 했다고 했어 | | 했다고 안 했어 | 했다고 했어? |
| I asked you | | I didn't ask you | Did you ask me? |
| 했냐고 물어봤어 | | 했냐고 묻지 않았어 | 했냐고 물어봤어? |
| I thought | | I didn't know | Did you know? |
| 한 줄 알았어 | | 한 줄 몰랐어 | 한 줄 알았어? |

## say & who's to say

배운 내용을 생각하며, 직접 문장을 만들어보세요!

정답확인 : P 283

| | |
|---|---|
| 01 | (너) 무슨 말이든 해도 돼. (아무거나 말해도 돼) 그래도 돼? |
| 02 | 고맙다고 말하고 싶었어.<br>-나도. |
| 03 | 너 가만히 있으면 안 돼. (뭐라고 해야 돼) |
| 04 | 내 말이! (너 그 말 다시 해도 돼!) [내 말이. You can say that again.] |
| 05 | 알지. (더 이상 말하지 마) [알지 Say no more.] 이해해. |
| 06 | 나도 그 말 하려고 했는데. (나 막 그 말 하려고 했었어) |
| 07 | 내가 하고 싶은 말이 (뭔가) 있어. |
| 08 | 네가 아무 말도 하지 말라고 했잖아. |
| 09 | 난 네가 이거 안 좋아한다고 한 줄 알았어. |
| 10 | 내가 좀 전에 말했듯이, 그건 문제가 아니야.<br>[내가 좀 전에 말했듯이, 아까 말한 대로 as I was saying] |
| 11 | 난 말 다 했어. [말 다 하다, 모든 걸 말해주다 say it all] |
| 12 | 네가 그렇다면야. (네가 그렇게 말하면야) 좋으실 대로. (네가 말하는 뭐든지)<br>[네가 그렇다면야 If you say so.] |
| 13 | 난 아무 말도 안 했어. |
| 14 | 난 네가 아무 말도 안 했으면 좋겠어. |
| 15 | 아무 말 안 하려고 했었는데.<br>-나도. |

# Review

| | |
|---|---|
| 16 | **아무 말도 하지 마.** |
| 17 | **그 말이 아니었어.** (난 그 말 하고 있던 거 아니야) |
| 18 | **더 이상 할 말이 없다.** (할 말이 남은 게 없다) [남은 left] |
| 19 | **그게 맞다는 말이 아니야.** (난 그게 맞다고 말하는 게 아니야) |
| 20 | **아무 말도 안 해도 돼. 알아.** |
| 21 | **너 그런 말은 하지 마.** (하지 않는 게 좋겠다) |
| 22 | **난 아무 말도 못 했어.** |
| 23 | **너 여기 온 후로 말 한마디 안 했어.** [한마디 a word] <br> -그랬나? |
| 24 | **나라면 그런 말 안 해.** |
| 25 | **그거 지금 해! 또 말 안 할 거야.** |
| 26 | **그 애가 뭐라고 했는지 모르겠어.** |
| 27 | **미안. 그 말은 진심이 아니었어.** (그 말 하려던 의도가 아니었어) <br> [진심이다, 뜻/의도/의미하다 mean to] |
| 28 | **뭐라고?** |
| 29 | **내가 언제 그랬어?** |
| 30 | **(그거) 다시 말해줄래?** |

## say & who's to say

배운 내용을 생각하며, 직접 문장을 만들어보세요!

| 31 | 내가 뭔가 말해도 돼? |
|----|---|
| 32 | 뭐라고 할 거야? |
| 33 | 뭐라고 하려고 했었어? |
| 34 | 너 하고 싶은 말이 (아무거라도) 있니? |
| 35 | 내가 뭐라고 하길 바라? |
| 36 | 말도 안 돼! [말도 안 되는, 터무니없는 nonsense] 누가 그래? (누가 그랬어?) |
| 37 | 누가 그래? (누가 그런 말을 하고 다녀?) |
| 38 | 할 말이 뭐가 더 있어? [뭐가 더 (what else/more)] 난 할 말 (아무것도) 없어. |
| 39 | 내가 뭐라고 하지? (뭐라고 하는 게 좋을까?) |
| 40 | 무슨 말이야? (너 지금 뭐라고 말하는 거야?) |
| 41 | 왜 그거 진작 말하지 않았어? [진작, 더 빨리 sooner] |
| 42 | 내가 뭐라고 해. (내가 무슨 말을 할 수 있겠어?) |
| 43 | 하고 싶은 말 다 했어? (그게 네가 말해야 되는 전부야?) |
| 44 | 무엇이 옳고 무엇이 그른지 누가 말할 수 있겠어? <br> [누가 말/장담/확신할 수 있겠어 who's to say] |
| 45 | 어떤 게 좋은지 나쁜지 누가 말할 수 있겠어? (무엇이 좋은지 아니면 나쁜지) |

# Dialogue Practice

**Regrets in Life**

A: What are the things that you regret in your life?

B: I regret caring too much about what others think.
   I thought they mattered.

A: Yeah, I understand.
   It's hard not to care about others' opinions.

B: I regret working too much.
   I thought work was the number 1 priority.

A: Ah, yeah. Work-life balance is so important.

B: I regret spending too much time worrying.
   I thought I couldn't help it.

**A**: What are the things you regret not doing?

**B**: I regret not traveling more.
I thought I would have time later.

**A**: Yeah. I agree. We all think we will have time later, don't we?

**B**: I regret not pursuing my passions.
I didn't think I could pursue my dreams.

**A**: Thank you. I should remember that.

**B**: I regret not spending enough time with my family and friends. I thought I was doing my best.
I also regret not showing them how much I loved them. This is very important. I would do it every day if I were you.

**A**: Thank you for sharing your wisdom.

# Dialogue Practice

_____ **Regrets in Life**

**A:** (당신의) 인생에서 후회하는 게 어떤 것들이 있어요?
[것들 the things]

**B:** 다른 사람들이 무슨 생각을 하는지에 너무 많이 신경 쓴 것을 후회해요.
[후회하다 regret -ing 신경 쓰다 care 다른 사람들 others]
전 (그들이) 중요한 줄 알았어요. [중요하다 matter]

**A:** 네, 이해해요.
다른 사람들의 의견들에 대해 신경 쓰지 않는 게 힘들죠.
[~않는 게 힘든 hard not to]

**B:** 일을 너무 많이 한거 후회해요.
일이 1순위인 줄 알았어요. [일 work 1순위 the number 1 priority]

**A:** 아, 네. 워라밸이 정말 중요하죠.
[워라밸, 일과 삶의 균형 work-life balance]

**B:** 걱정하는데 너무 많은 시간을 보낸 것을 후회해요.
[시간을 보내다 spend (too much) time -ing]
어쩔 수 없는 줄 알았어요. [어쩔 수 없다 can't help it]

**A**: 하지 않은 것을 후회하는 것은 어떤 것들이 있어요?
[하지 않은 것들 not doing]

**B**: 여행을 더 하지 않은 것을 후회해요.
나중에 시간이 있을 줄 알았어요.

**A**: 네, 동의해요.
우린 모두 나중에 시간이 있을 거라고 생각하지요, 그렇죠?

**B**: 제 열정들을 추구하지 않은 것을 후회해요.
[열정을 추구하다 pursue one's passion(s)]
전 제 꿈들을 추구할 수 없을 것 같았어요.

**A**: 고마워요. 그걸 기억해야겠어요. (기억하는 게 좋겠어요)

**B**: 제 가족이랑 친구들과 충분한 시간을 보내지 않은 것을 후회해요. 전 최선을 다하고 있는 줄 알았어요.
전 그들에게 (제가 그들을) 얼마큼 사랑하는지 보여주지 않은 것 또한 후회해요. 이게 매우 중요해요. 내가 당신이라면 매일 하겠어요.

**A**: (당신의) 지혜를 나누어주셔서 감사합니다. [지혜 wisdom]

정/답/체/크

# 정답 체크

## Unit 1

1. I want to (/would like to) go out and do something.
   -So do (/would) I. What shall we do?
2. I'm so tired.
   -So am I. We should call it a night.
3. I like this.
   -So do I. We have so much in common.
4. I have to leave early.
   -So do we. What time are you going to leave?
5. I was so happy to see you.
   -So was I.
6. I enjoyed it so much. I had a great/good time.
   -So did I. It was so good.
7. I have been there many times.
   -So have I. That's my favorite spot.
8. I know.
   -So do I.
9. We were late.
   -So was I. Everyone was late.
10. I can fix it.
    -So can I. Do you want to do it or should I?
11. I'm so excited about our new project.
    -So am I. It's promising.
12. I used to love/like this when I was little (/a child/a kid). (I liked it when I was little.)
    -So did I.
13. I want to (/would like to) watch/see this movie.
    -So do (/would) I. Let's see/watch this (one), shall we?
14. I was going to choose/pick this.
    -So was I. Everyone wanted this.
15. I've already seen it. (I saw it already.)
    -So have I. (So did I.)
16. I want to (/would like to) go to South America one day.
    -So do (/would) I.
    Which part of South America do you want to (/would you like to) travel (to)?
17. I can wait as long as it takes.
    -So can I. Bring it on!
18. I went to the movies last night.
    -So did I. What movie did you see?

19. I would do it if I were him.
    -So would I. I just don't understand him.
20. I'd like to (/want to) meet him.
    -So would (/do) I.
21. I'm sorry. I was wrong.
    -So was I. You don't have to apologize.
22. I wanted to say thank you.
    -So did I. And thank you for saying that.
23. I was going to help him.
    -So were we. It was too late.
24. I have been meaning to call him.
    -So have I. I just haven't had (the) time.
25. I was hungry.
    -So was I.
26. I totally forgot about that.
    -So did I.
27. I have time to kill.
    -So do I.
28. I've known him for a long time.
    -So have I. It's been about 10 years.
29. I'll think about it.
    -So will I. Let's sleep on it, shall we?
30. I miss him so much.
    -So do I. And so does everyone.
31. You look good/nice/great today.
    -So do you!
32. You're so beautiful.
    -So are you.
33. You did a great/good job.
    -So did you. It was a good game.
34. You were amazing!
    -So were you. I'm so proud of you.
35. I should (/have to) get back to work. And so should (/do) you.
36. You look tired.
    -So do you.
37. You lied to me.
    -So did you.
38. You have been working hard. (You worked hard.)
    -So has everyone. (So did everyone.)

## 정답 체크

39. I think he'll be interested.
    -So do I.
40. He'll love/like it when he tries it. And so will you.
41. I can do it easily, and so can you.
42. He'll help you. And so will I.
43. Yes, I did it. And so did you.
44. He has it. And so do I. You can borrow it any time.
45. Your father's worried about you. And so am I.
46. He was crying. And so was I. It was heartbreaking.
47. He thinks you are wonderful. And so do I. Don't forget that.
48. I was there. And so was he.
49. Mary likes/loves this. And so does her husband.
50. He's a great/good cook, and so is Peter.
51. I don't know anything about it.
    -Neither do I.
52. I'm not angry.
    -Neither am I.
53. I can't remember.
    -Neither can I.
54. I'm not going to go there.
    -Neither am I.
55. I didn't say anything.
    -Neither did I.
56. I haven't told anyone.
    -Neither have I.
57. I couldn't say anything.
    -Neither could I.
58. I haven't been there for ages.
    -Neither have I.
59. I'm not kidding/joking.
    -Neither am I. I'm dead serious.
60. I don't like it.
    -Neither do I.
61. I don't want to (/wouldn't like to) go.
    -Neither do (/would) I, but we have to.
62. I didn't want to do that.
    -Neither did I.
63. I haven't been there.
    -Neither have I.

64. I wasn't tired at all.
    -Neither was I.
65. I can't do this alone.
    -Neither can I. We should do it together.
66. I don't think he'll come.
    -Neither do I.
67. I won't tell anyone.
    -Neither will I. I promise.
68. I couldn't finish it.
    -Neither could I. There wasn't enough time.
69. I wouldn't do that.
    -Neither would I. It might/may ruin everything.
70. I didn't do it.
    -Neither did I.
71. I can't wait that long.
    -Neither can I.
72. I haven't thought about that.
    -Neither have I.
73. I didn't use this.
    -Neither did I.
74. I don't have to work tomorrow.
    -Neither do I. Do you want to (/Would you like to) do something together?
75. I'm not going to change my mind.
    -Neither am I.
76. It was (so) terrible. I didn't like it.
    -Neither did I.
77. I'm not doing much now.
    -Neither am I. Do you want to (/Would you like to) grab a coffee?
78. I don't think it'll work.
    -Neither do I. What should we do?
79. I wasn't ready.
    -Neither was I. Frankly, nobody was (ready).
80. I didn't know.
    -Neither did I. I feel so bad.
81. I don't have time for this.
    -Neither do I. We shouldn't waste any more time.
82. I haven't had any problems so far.
    -Neither have I.

## 정답 체크

83. I'm not ready to get married.
    -Neither am I.
84. I didn't use to like this.
    -Neither did I. It grew (/has grown) on me.
85. I don't see it that way.
    -Neither do I. We are on the same page.
86. I couldn't sleep at all last night.
    -Neither could I.
87. I don't mind waiting.
    -Neither do we.
88. You shouldn't blame yourself.
    -I know. Neither should you.
89. I don't know them well enough.
    -Neither do I.
90. I can't understand what he's saying.
    -Neither can I. He's talking nonsense.
91. He doesn't need this, and neither do you.
92. You shouldn't be here, and neither should he.
93. He isn't going to say anything, and neither am I.
94. He doesn't eat this, and neither does Jim.
95. They don't have to bring anything, and neither do you.
96. Nick isn't here. And neither is Sue.
97. I wasn't happy about that, and neither was Kelly.
98. He doesn't want to do anything, and neither do I.
99. That phone's not working, and neither is this (one).
    (That phone doesn't work, and neither does this one.)
100. I'll never talk about it again from this day forward. And neither will you. Got it?

### Review

1. I want to (/would like to) believe you.
2. You have to believe me. I'm telling you the truth.
3. It's so hard to believe, isn't it?
4. I believed him. I'm such a fool.
5. It might/may be hard to believe, but I really like it.
6. You can believe him.
7. Everyone's going to (/will) believe it.
8. I'll believe it when I see it.

9. Believe it or not, it's the truth.
10. He doesn't believe me.
11. I didn't believe him.
    -Neither did I.
12. It was hard to believe. I couldn't believe my eyes.
13. Don't believe everything you hear. It might/may not be true.
14. You can't believe everything he says.
15. I don't know what to believe anymore.
16. I don't think he'll believe the story.
17. I don't think we should believe him.
18. Nobody is going to (/will) believe you.
19. You don't have to believe me. See for yourself!
20. I'm not going to believe him again.
21. I wouldn't believe him if I were you.
22. I can't believe what you're saying. Are you out of your mind?
23. You might/may not believe me. But it's true.
24. Do you believe me now?
25. Do you think I should believe him?
26. Why is it so hard to believe?
27. Can I believe you? How can I believe you?
28. Did you believe him?
29. Why should I believe you?
30. Do you think he'll believe me?
31. What should I believe?
32. He's not coming. Can you believe it?
33. I used to believe in God, but not anymore.
34. He believes in you. And so do I.
35. I've always believed in you. I knew you could do it.
36. He's always believed in me. Even when I didn't believe in myself.
37. I would believe in myself.
38. Thank you for believing in me.
39. I didn't use to believe in miracles. Miracles (do) happen.
40. Do you believe in love?

## Unit 2

1. I can call you back later if you're busy now.
   -Can you? Thank you. I'll talk to you later.
2. It'll be ready (by) tomorrow. You can pick it up then.
   -Can I? That's good news.
3. You have to change your password at least every six months.
   -Do I?
4. I want to (/would like to) get to know you better.
   -Do you? (/Would you?) What do you want to (/would you like to) know?
5. Don't worry about it. I'll help you with it.
   -Will you? You're the best.
6. I think it'll get easier with time.
   -Do you? I really hope so.
7. You should make up your mind.
   -Should I? But I don't know what I want.
8. I think you should do this.
   -Do you? Do you think I can do it?
9. Everything's going to (/will) be okay/fine.
   -Is (/Will) it? Are you sure?
10. I'm going to go out/leave now.
    -Are you? When are you going to be/come back?
11. It costs a lot to do that.
    -Does it? Why does it cost so much?
12. It took a while to get used to the new environment.
    -Did it? How long did it take?
13. I used to like that, but not anymore.
    -Did you?
14. It's going to (/will) be easy.
    -Is (/Will) it? I'm still worried.
15. You're more than welcome to come.
    -Am I? Thank you so much.
16. He cried and cried and cried.
    -Did he? Why did he cry?
17. You can take it.
    -Can I? Thank you.
18. There's plenty. (There're plenty.)
    -Is there? (Are there?)

19. I have been there.
    -Have you? When did you go there?
20. I was driving then.
    -Were you? Where were you going?
21. It's so important to me.
    -Is it? Why is that?
22. You're so talented.
    -Am I? You're not just saying that, are you?
23. He's great/good at it.
    -Is he? I didn't know.
24. I want to (/would like to) buy it in every color!
    -Do (/Would) you? I do that, too. If(/When) I love/like it (/something), I buy it in every color.
25. If you love/like it, you should get/buy it.
    -Should I? I really want to.
26. It was freezing cold.
    -Was it?
27. I've decided to do it. (I decided to do it.)
    -Have you? (Did you?) That's good. I support whatever decision you make.
28. I have been working (/I have worked) there for almost 5 years.
    -Have you? Has it already been 5 years?
29. I was going to tell you.
    -Were you? When were you going to do that?
30. I need a favor.
    -Do you? What is it? What can I do for you?
31. You did great/well.
    -Did I? Thank you. You're so sweet.
32. I knew it already. (I already knew it.)
    -Did you? How did you find out?
33. We had so much fun.
    -Did you? I'm so happy to hear that.
34. They've known each other for ages/a long time.
    -Have they?
35. Stop lying. He told me everything.
    -Did he? What did he say exactly?
36. They're convenient to use.
    -Are they?

## 정답 체크

37. They have just arrived. (They just arrived.)
    -Have they? (Did they?)
38. I wanted to ask you something.
    -Did you? What was it?
39. I didn't know where you were. I was so worried about you.
    -Were you? I'm so sorry.
40. I know what you are going to say.
    -Do you? What am I going to say?
41. I like/love my job.
    -Do you? What do you like most about your job?
42. It was crowded. There were so many people.
    -Were there?
43. I got rid of it.
    -Did you? When did you do that?
44. I want to (/would like to) ask you something.
    -Do (/Would) you? What is it?
45. I was waving at you.
    -Were you? I didn't see you.
46. It was so annoying.
    -Was it? I feel you. I hate it too when people do that.
47. I'll do it later.
    -Will you? Thanks.
48. There's something I have to do.
    -Is there? Do you have to go now?
49. You have to come.
    -Do I? Do I really have to?
50. I was going to do that.
    -Were you? I don't believe you.
51. I'm hungry.
    -Are you? Would you like (/Do you want) something to eat?
52. I forgot to do that.
    -Did you? You can do it now.
53. It's been so stressful.
    -Has it?
54. Sorry, I'm distracted.
    -Are you? Is something bothering you?
55. We decided not to do that. (We've decided not to do that.)
    -Did you? (Have you?) What are you going to do?

56. It used to be my favorite.
    -Did it?
57. We're working together.
    -Are you?
58. He designs logos.
    -Does he?
59. There is something we can do for him.
    -Is there? What can we do?
60. I have been working out/exercising.
    -Have you? You look great/good.
61. It isn't there.
    -Isn't it? I wonder where it is.
62. I don't know what else to do.
    -Don't you? That's understandable.
63. It doesn't matter.
    -Doesn't it? Are you sure?
64. It wasn't here.
    -Wasn't it? Where did it go? (Where has it gone?)
65. I haven't been there yet.
    -Haven't you?
66. I couldn't do it.
    -Couldn't you? When can you do it, then?
67. I wasn't expecting you.
    -Weren't you? I told you yesterday.
68. He doesn't like this.
    -Doesn't he?
69. You don't have to do it.
    -Don't I?
70. There wasn't (/weren't) enough.
    -Wasn't (/Weren't) there?
71. You are not going to (/won't) like it.
    -Aren't (/Won't) I?
72. I wasn't paying attention.
    -Weren't you? What were you thinking about?
73. It doesn't look safe.
    -Doesn't it?
74. I haven't slept well for a few days.
    -Haven't you?

## 정답 체크

75. It didn't hurt.
    -Didn't it?
76. We shouldn't take it.
    -Shouldn't we?
77. I don't think he'll come.
    -Don't you? Is he busy?
78. I haven't brought it. (I didn't bring it.)
    -Haven't you? (Didn't you?) Don't worry. I'll lend it to you.
79. I didn't do anything. (I haven't done anything.)
    -Didn't you? (Haven't you?)
80. We can't leave/go out yet.
    -Can't we? When can we leave/go out?
81. I'm not going home.
    -Aren't you? Where are you going?
82. It won't be there.
    -Won't it? Where do you think it is?
83. I wasn't going to go there.
    -Weren't you? Why did you go?
84. I didn't mean to hurt you.
    -Didn't you? I know.
85. I don't think it'll be that hard.
    -Don't you? I'm relieved.
86. There isn't anything (/is nothing) you have to worry about.
    -Isn't there? I hope you're right.
87. You haven't given me the change yet.
    -Haven't I? I'm sorry.
88. It wasn't your fault.
    -Wasn't it? It doesn't feel like it.
89. When I was little (/a child/a kid), I didn't (use to) like it.
    -Didn't you?
90. I wouldn't say that.
    -Wouldn't you? What would you say?
91. You can't cancel it now.
    -Can't I?
92. There aren't many people here.
    -Aren't there? How many people are there?
93. It wasn't easy to convince him.
    -Wasn't it?

94. We shouldn't take that.
    -Shouldn't we?
95. You haven't done anything wrong. (You didn't do anything wrong.)
    -Haven't I? (Didn't I?)
96. It hasn't been long.
    -Hasn't it? It feels like forever.
97. I'm not ashamed.
    -Aren't you? You shouldn't be (ashamed) anyway.
98. I wouldn't do that.
    -Wouldn't you? What would you do?
99. He didn't tell me anything.
    -Didn't he? Then, how did you know?
100. I don't know what I have to do now.
    -Don't you?


**Review**

1. You have to know.
2. I want to (/I'd like to) know everything about you.
3. He might/may know.
4. I knew it. I knew it would happen.
   -Did you?
5. I used to know everything about him. We used to be so close.
6. He knows about everything.
7. Everyone is going to (/will) know. I don't want that.
8. I've known it for a while.
   -Have you? How did you find out?
9. No. I should know better.
10. No, I'm not going to do it. I know better.
11. You'll know it when you see it.
    -Will I?
12. There's no way to know for sure.
13. It's good to know. Thank you for telling me.
14. You know me so well, don't you?
15. He'll know.
16. I would know.
17. I'm dying to know.
18. It'll be over before you know it.

## 정답 체크

19. As far as I know, there's no problem (/there isn't a problem).
20. I don't want to know. (I wouldn't like to know.)
21. He doesn't know anything, does he?
22. I didn't know about that.
    −Didn't you?
23. He can't know about this.
24. He doesn't have to know.
25. I wouldn't know what to do.
26. We can't know for sure.
27. I don't know what I'm going to (/will) do without you.
28. No one will know.
29. They may/might not know anything yet.
30. Not knowing is better than knowing sometimes.
31. Is knowing better than not knowing? What do you think?
32. What do you want to (/would you like to) know?
33. What do you know? How much do you know?
34. How long have you known each other?
35. Did you know about this?
36. How can I know for sure?
37. Do I have to know?
38. Do you think he'll know?
39. When can we know for sure?
40. Do you know much about cars?
41. He's such a know-it-all.
42. You're a little know-it-all, aren't you?
43. He used to be a know-it-all.
44. I'm not a know-it-all.
45. People don't like know-it-alls.

## Unit 3

1. Who knows? You might/may be lucky.
2. Who knew? It was totally unexpected.
3. Who gave you this? (Who gave it to you?) Where did you get it?
4. Who did this? Do you know who did it?
5. Who's doing this?
6. Who will/would do that? Nobody will/would.
7. Who would/will do such a thing?
8. Who said that?
9. Who told you that? That's not true.

10. Who asked you that question? Do you remember who did?
11. Who called?
12. Who's calling you at this hour?
13. Who's going to (/will) call him? He has nobody. (He doesn't have anyone.)
14. Who hates that? Everybody likes it.
15. Who found this? Can you tell me who found it?
16. Who broke it? Did you see who broke it?
17. Who took my book?
18. Who's going to take you there? Shall I give you a ride?
19. Who's coming to the party? How many people are coming?
20. Did someone come here while I was out? Who came?
21. What's going on? Why is everyone here?
22. What was the problem?
23. What's the matter?
24. What went wrong? I want to (/would like to) know where it went wrong.
25. Do you have a problem with your phone? What is wrong with it?
26. Is it working now? What was wrong with it?
27. What seems to be the problem?
28. What's in it?
29. Was something in there? What was in it?
30. What changed? What changed your mind?
31. What will (/is going to) happen to him?
32. What (has) happened to him? Nobody has heard from him since he left last week.
33. What happened to you earlier?
34. What happened to your lips?
35. What's happening to me? Everything's happening so fast.
36. What brings you here? I've never seen you here before.
   (I haven't seen you here before.)
37. What brought you here?
38. It's smoky in here. What's burning?
39. What's on your nose?
40. What took you so long? Where have you been all these years?
   I've been waiting for you all my life.
41. Who brought this in here? You cannot/can't bring anything in here.
42. Did anyone/someone see you? Who saw you?
43. Who has time for that? It's a waste of time.
44. Who had time to do that? There was no time. (There wasn't time.)
45. Who did this to you? Who hit you?
46. Who won the game? Who was the winner?

## 정답 체크

47. Who made these?
48. Who put this here? Was it you?
49. Who taught you that? Was it self-taught?
50. Who sent you this? (Who sent it to you?) Do you know who did?
51. What makes you sad?
52. What made you cry?
53. What makes you say that?
54. What makes you think like that? It makes me so sad.
55. What made you change your mind?
56. What makes you happy? Can you tell me 5 things that make you happy?
57. What makes you so sure?
58. What's all this? What gives?
59. What gave you that idea?
60. What gave you that impression?
61. Who sold that to you? (Who sold you that?)
62. Is someone here? Who's there?
63. I didn't tell anybody. (I haven't told anyone.)
    -Neither did I. (Neither have I.) Then, who did?
64. Who does that? (Who would do that?) It's unspeakable.
65. Who ate my cake?
66. Who likes that? Nobody does.
67. Who would/will want that?
68. Who would/will want to go out with me? I feel unattractive.
69. Who went to the hospital with you? You didn't go alone, did you?
70. Who ordered this? Whose is this?
71. Which one was it? Was it the red one?
72. Which one costs more?
73. Which one will (/is going to) take less time?
74. Which part was your favorite?
75. What's the best movie you've ever seen?
76. What caused the accident?
77. How many people came to the conference?
78. How many people will attend the seminar?
79. How many people (have) switched to the new service?
80. Who gives a shit/crap? (Who cares?) Nobody cares. (Nobody does.)
81. Who's fixing it?
82. Who used mine?
83. Who wrote this? Did you write it?
84. Who gave you that advice? That's wise advice.
85. Who lives in that house?

86. I don't know who used to live in that house, but I know who's living (/who lives) there now.
87. Who's responsible for this? Whose responsibility is that?
88. Who's going to (/will) believe you?
89. What's the best thing that has happened to you in your life?
90. What's stopping you? Why are you (being) indecisive?
91. What kind of jobs interest you?
92. Who inspired you to do that?
93. Who likes this?
94. Who has a pen?
95. Who knows the answer?
96. Who wants to eat something?
97. Who likes wine?
98. Who wants to be on my team?
99. Who wants to be a millionaire?
100. Whose phone (still) has a signal?

**Review**

1. We used to come here every day. It was (/used to be) our favorite spot.
2. He comes here every Friday.
   -Does he?
3. I came/got here 5 minutes ago. I've been here for 5 minutes.
4. You have to come. We're going to (/will) have a good time together.
5. You can come if you have time.
6. I've been here many times before.
7. I think he'll come.
8. I think you should come, too.
9. He was coming home.
10. He might/may come. I don't know.
11. He's coming. He'll (/is going to) be/come here soon.
12. I was going to come, but I couldn't.
13. I have been coming here for 6 months.
14. You might as well come, too.
15. You want to come, don't you? (You'd like to come, wouldn't you?)
16. I've always wanted to come here.
    -So have I.
17. Come and give me a kiss, will you?
18. I don't think he should come.

## 정답 체크

19. I don't know if/whether he'll come.
20. I haven't been here for ages.
21. You didn't want to come, did you?
22. You don't have to come if you don't want to.
23. I don't think he'll come.
    -Don't you?
24. Sorry, I couldn't come to your party yesterday.
25. They might/may not come.
26. I wouldn't come here, either.
27. Don't come here again.
28. He wasn't going to come.
    -Wasn't he?
29. Success doesn't come easy. Easy come, easy go.
30. He can't come. I don't want to (/wouldn't like to) see him.
31. He's not going to come, is he? (He won't come, will he?)
32. It didn't come naturally to me. I had to work hard for it.
33. I don't know why I came here.
34. When did you come (/get here)?
35. How long have you been here?
36. What time do you want to (/would you like to) come?
37. When do I have to come?
38. When do you think you'll come?
39. How often does he come here?
40. What time shall I come?
41. Is Mom coming, too?
42. Can (/Could/May) I come, too?
43. When do you think I should come?
44. Who's going to (/will/would) come?
45. It comes with a gift bag.
46. The dish comes with a salad.
47. It came with soup.
48. Does it come with fries?

## Unit 4

1. Isn't this bigger than that (one)?
   -No, it isn't. I don't think so. It's smaller.
2. Don't we have to go now?
   -Yes, we do. Are you ready?

3. Aren't you going to say something?
   -No, I'm not going to say anything.
4. Don't you want to go?
   -Yes, I do. But I don't know if/whether I have time.
5. Can't we go now?
   -No, we can't. We have to wait for Jim.
6. Isn't this yours?
   -Yes, it is (mine). Thank you. I have been (/was) looking for it.
7. Haven't you done it yet?
   -No, I haven't (done it yet).
8. Don't you have it?
   -No, I don't. Can (/Could/May) I borrow yours?
9. Didn't you say something?
   -No, I didn't say anything.
10. Wasn't it good?
    -Yes, it was (good). I had a good/nice/great time.
11. Don't you like this?
    -Yes, I do. Thanks for the gift.
12. Didn't you hear something?
    -No, I didn't. What did you hear?
13. Isn't it a beautiful day today?
    -Yes, it is.
14. Haven't we met before?
    -Yes, we have.
15. Wasn't it an accident?
    -Yes, it was.
16. Doesn't it have to be similar?
    -No, not really.
17. These look the same. Aren't they the same?
    -No, they aren't. They're all different.
18. Didn't I pay for this?
    -Yes, you did.
19. Didn't I tell you?
    -No, you didn't. So, what happened next?
20. Aren't you tired?
    -No, I'm fine/okay. Thank you for caring.
21. Don't I have to bring something/anything?
    -No, you don't. Just bring yourself.

## 정답 체크

22. Doesn't it cost a lot (of money) to do that?
    -No, it doesn't.
23. Wasn't it expensive to fix?
    -Yes, it was. It cost a lot (of money).
24. Didn't it take long to go/get there?
    -Yes, it did. It took 2 hours.
25. Weren't you looking for this? (Haven't you been looking for this?)
    -Yes, you're right. Where did you find it?
26. Don't you go there often?
    -No, I don't. I used to, but I haven't been there for a long time.
27. Didn't you use to have that?
    -Yes, I did.
28. Isn't it hard/difficult to do that sometimes?
    -Yes, it is.
29. Weren't you going to do this?
    -Yes, I was. But I didn't have time.
30. Can't he eat this?
    -No, he can't. He's allergic to nuts.
31. Aren't you busy now?
    -Yes, I am. But I always have time for you.
32. Haven't you been there?
    -No, I haven't. I want to (/would like to) someday.
33. Wasn't it fun?
    -Yes, it was. It was so much fun.
34. Doesn't he look different?
    -Yes, he does. He's like a different person.
35. Didn't he sound upset?
    -No, he didn't. He sounded okay/fine.
36. Isn't it better to wait? (Shouldn't we wait?)
    -Yes, it is. (Yes, we should.) We should wait until we know for sure.
37. Weren't you hungry?
    -Yes, I was. I was starving.
38. Can't you be more careful?
    -Sorry, I will be more careful.
39. Shouldn't we do something about it?
    -Yes (we should), but I don't know what we should do.
40. Isn't he adorable?
    -Yes, he is. He's so cute.

41. Doesn't he like this?
    -Yes, he does.
42. Aren't you going to go there?
    -No, I'm not. I don't want to (/wouldn't like to), this time.
43. Wasn't it there?
    -No, it wasn't. I looked everywhere, but I couldn't find it.
44. Don't you agree with me? Don't you think so?
    -Yes, I do.
45. Can't you do it today?
    -Sorry, I can't do it today.
46. Don't you have to hurry?
    -Yes, I do. I lost track of time. Thanks for reminding me.
47. Did it cost more? Wasn't it 40 dollars?
    -No, it wasn't. It cost more.
48. Don't you want to go with me?
    -Yes, I do.
49. Isn't it so nice/good?
    -Yes, it is.
50. Weren't you going to say something?
    -No, I wasn't.
51. Didn't you know?
    -No, I didn't.
52. Isn't there enough time?
    -Yes, there is.
53. Aren't you going to do this?
    -Yes, I am. I'm going to (/will) do it when I go/get home.
54. Wasn't it hard?
    -No, it wasn't. It wasn't too bad.
55. Hasn't it been long?
    -Yes (it has), it has been so long.
56. Shouldn't we go home now?
    -Yes, we should.
57. Aren't you coming?
    -Yes, I am coming.
58. Aren't you supposed to be at work? (Shouldn't you be at work?)
    -No, (I'm not) it's my day off. I told you yesterday.
59. Aren't you supposed to be taking notes?
60. Aren't we supposed to be helping him?
61. Why can't he understand?

## 정답 체크

62. Why didn't you come?
    -Sorry, something came up at the last minute.
63. Why don't you understand me? It makes me sad.
64. Why isn't he coming?
    -I think he's busy.
65. Why didn't you talk/speak to me? Don't I matter?
66. Why doesn't it work? (Why isn't it working?)
    -I don't know. It's been like that for a few days.
67. Why didn't you do it? Didn't you want to do it?
68. Why didn't you say anything?
    -I just couldn't.
69. Why didn't you tell me?
    -Sorry, I was going to, but I forgot.
70. Why isn't it here? Have you seen it? (Did you see it?)
71. Why can't he trust you?
72. Why didn't he go to work?
73. Why aren't you working now? Aren't you supposed to be working?
74. Why don't you like this?
75. Why don't you want to go?
76. Why wasn't I aware of this? Why didn't you tell me sooner?
77. Why didn't anyone tell me about this?
78. Why weren't you surprised? Did you know it would happen?
79. Who hasn't been there? It's so famous. Everyone has been there.
80. Who doesn't like peace and quiet once in a while?
81. Do you not remember?
    -No, I don't.
82. Can you not believe me?
    -Yes, I can.
83. Did you not hear me?
    -No, I didn't. Sorry.
84. Is it not enough?
    -Yes, it is.
85. Am I not good enough for you?
86. Was I not (good) enough for him?
87. Have you not read that book?
88. Do you not want to stay here?
89. Can you not eat this?
90. Can you not say that (, please)?
91. Why don't you sit down?

92. Why don't I go and get some water for you?
93. Why don't we take five?
94. Why don't you have time to think about it, and let me know when you're ready? I can wait.
95. Why don't I show you how to do that?
96. Why don't we have a meeting tomorrow afternoon?
97. Why don't you give it a try? There's nothing (/isn't anything) to lose.
98. Why don't we pretend nothing happened? Just act normal.
99. Why don't we make a deal? If I do this for you, you do something for me in return.
100. Why don't you let me worry about it? There's no need to worry.


**Review**

1. I think you should stay here.
2. If you stay, I'll stay.
3. He might/may stay longer.
4. He stays with us when he comes to Korea.
5. You have to stay for dinner.
6. You can stay here.
   –Can I?
7. He's going to (/will) stay with us for a while.
8. It stayed with me for a long time. I couldn't get it out of my head.
9. I was going to stay there, but I changed my mind.
10. I've been staying here since Monday.
11. I used to stay at my friend's place/house whenever I was in (/went to) Japan.
12. I want to (/I'd like to) know how long he'll (/is going to) stay here.
13. I want to stay here. (I'd like to stay here.)
    –So do I. (So would I.)
14. You might as well stay here.
15. I can't stay here.
    –Neither can I.
16. You weren't staying there, were you?
17. I couldn't stay there any longer.
18. Everything changes. Nothing stays the same.
19. I haven't found a place to stay yet.
20. Can (/Could/May) I stay here for a few days?
21. I didn't want to stay there.
    –Didn't you?
22. I don't think we should stay here.

## 정답 체크

23. I don't want to (/wouldn't like to) overstay my welcome.
24. I wouldn't overstay my welcome.
25. He might/may not stay here. He might/may find somewhere else.
26. You aren't staying with your friends, are you?
27. We don't have to stay here if you don't want to.
28. Where do you want to (/would you like to) stay?
29. Where are you going to stay? How long are you going to stay there?
30. Where did you stay?
31. Do we have to stay here?
32. Where do you think you'll stay?
33. Can (/Could) we stay here?
34. Where were you going to stay?
35. Do you know where he's staying?
36. How long have you been staying here?
37. Didn't you stay at a hotel?
38. Don't you want to stay here?
39. Who stayed here?
40. Where does he stay when he goes to China?
41. Is there somewhere you can stay?
42. Stay in touch, will you?
43. We stayed in touch for a few years. And we lost contact.
44. I would like to (/want to) stay in touch with you.
45. We met in 2008 when I went to Japan. We've been staying in touch ever since.

## Unit 5

1. When we got/went there, the movie had already started.
2. When I arrived, they had already closed. So, I couldn't buy anything.
3. When I got/came home, everyone had gone to bed.
4. When Jim arrived there, Sue had already left.
5. When I got up, he had already left for work.
6. We saw a/the movie together. But I had seen it before.
7. I went to Inchoen. We had wanted to go to Kang-won Province, but we (had) decided not to.
8. I got this for my birthday. I had always wanted to have it.
9. I was so upset when I lost it. I had had it for a long time. It had sentimental value for me.
10. I sold my old car last year. I had driven it for nearly 10 years.

11. Last weekend was relaxing. I had been so busy, and I had needed that.
12. It was a blast. I had so much fun. I had forgotten what fun was.
13. I knew it already. Somebody had told me.
14. I knew (that). You had already said that.
15. I was aware of it. You had warned me. Don't you remember?
16. I didn't want to go, because I had been there many times.
17. I had booked the tickets in advance.
    –So had I. I knew it would be hard to get them/the tickets.
18. I had done it before Jim did.
19. I had arrived before everyone came. I was the first one to arrive.
20. I couldn't speak/talk to him. He had left before I could (speak/talk to him).
21. It wasn't my first time. I had done it before.
    –So had I.
22. He left the firm last month. He had been working (/had worked) there for 15 years.
23. It wasn't easy to leave him. We had been together for 5 years.
24. I watched/saw the movie again. I had watched/seen it before. But I had wanted to see/watch it again.
25. I couldn't find it. Even though I had looked everywhere.
26. I was late for the meeting because I had missed the train.
27. I didn't have to tell him. He had already known.
28. We were good friends. We had known each other since we were maybe 5.
29. It was such a mess. He had done so much damage.
30. He was crying uncontrollably. Something had happened to him.
31. I knew something bad had happened to him.
32. He was a hero. He had done great things in life.
33. He had taught me so much. I still miss him.
34. I had learned so much from him. He was my role model.
35. You knew what I had wanted, didn't you?
36. I knew what he had needed, but I couldn't give it to him.
37. I didn't realize what I had done until it was too late.
38. I didn't realize what he had meant to me.
39. I didn't know where he had gone. He hadn't told me anything.
40. I didn't know if/whether I had done the right thing.
41. I felt like I had forgotten something.
42. I had to go back home. Because I had forgotten to bring the documents.
43. I didn't eat anything because I had eaten a big lunch.
44. I felt sick. Because I had had/eaten too much ice cream.
45. I had heard that so many times before.

## 정답 체크

46. I had read the book before I watched/saw the movie.
47. He was upset. He had lost his ring.
48. There was nothing (/wasn't anything) left to do. I had done everything I could.
49. No one knew what I had been/gone through. I hadn't told anyone.
50. I couldn't remember what you had said.
51. It was so good to see him. We hadn't seen each other for a long time.
52. I didn't know who Wendy was. I hadn't met her before.
53. When I went there to pick it up, they hadn't fixed my car.
    I have to go back there again today.
54. I was so hungry. I hadn't eaten/had anything since breakfast.
55. It was so good. I hadn't been there before. It was my first time.
56. I was surprised. I hadn't expected anything.
57. I trusted/believed him. He hadn't lied to me before.
58. I wasn't expecting that. I hadn't seen it coming.
59. It was so unfair! It wasn't my fault. I hadn't done anything wrong.
    (I had done nothing wrong.)
60. It was my first try. I hadn't done it before.
61. I had never been there before. I wanted to go somewhere I had never been before.
    (I wanted to go somewhere I hadn't been before)
62. It was so beautiful. I had never seen anything like that before.
63. It was incredible! I hadn't experienced anything like that before.
64. It was a new experience. I hadn't done anything like that before.
65. Everything was the same. Nothing had changed.
66. He looked the same. He hadn't changed a bit.
67. Everything was just fine. Nothing had happened.
68. Why did you pretend nothing had happened?
69. I think there was a problem. We had been there for an hour, and the show hadn't even started.
70. It was good to catch up. We hadn't spoken/talked to each other for a long time.
71. I didn't know about that. He hadn't told me anything.
72. I wasn't aware of it. No one had said anything.
73. That was the first time I had heard about it. You hadn't told me.
74. I hadn't realized it until you told me.
75. I left my phone at the shop. I hadn't realized it until I got home.
76. Really? I hadn't noticed.
77. It was right there, but I hadn't even noticed.
78. How did you come up with that? I hadn't even thought about that.
79. I hadn't even dreamed of it.
80. I hadn't even dreamed of getting another award.

81. Had you been here before, or was it your first time?
82. Had you seen it already? (Had you already seen it?)
83. Had he left anything for me before he left?
84. How long had you had that before you sold it?
85. Had you studied English before you went to Canada?
86. What had you done before you came here?
87. Where had you been that day?
88. Hadn't I done enough? I couldn't live like that any longer.
89. Hadn't you read the book before you watched/saw the movie?
90. What had happened before I came?
91. It finally came yesterday. I had been waiting for months.
92. Where were you? I had been calling you. (I had been trying to call you.)
93. I had been meaning to ask you about your weekend, but I kept forgetting.
94. It was a difficult time. We had been trying to have a baby for a long time.
95. He had been cheating (on her) for a year.
96. Apparently, it had been going on for years.
97. I was tired. I had been working all day.
98. I gave it away. I had had it for a long time, but I hadn't been using it.
99. I had just arrived before you came. I hadn't been waiting long.
100. What had you been doing that morning?

**Review**

1. I can hear you well. Stop yelling!
2. Yes, I (have) heard. How are you?
3. I have to hear your side of the story.
4. It's so nice to meet you. I've heard so much about you.
5. I want to (/would like to) hear all about it.
6. It's so nice/good to hear your voice. I'm glad/happy you called.
7. I look forward to hearing from you soon.
8. You'll (/are going to) hear from me soon.
9. This is the first time I'm hearing about this.
10. I've heard that many times before.
    -So have I.
11. I used to hear that a lot.
    -Did you?
12. It was good to hear from you.
13. You should hear it from him.
14. I've been hearing ringing in my ears.

## 정답 체크

15. I knew that. I had heard it from Kim.
16. I don't want to (/wouldn't like to) hear it.
17. I can't hear you. You're breaking up.
18. I don't hear anything.
19. I've never heard of it.
20. Okay, I'll tell you. But you didn't hear it from me.
21. You're not hearing me. That's not what I mean.
22. If you don't hear from me in 5 minutes, call the police/cops.
23. I didn't hear anything.
    -Didn't you?
24. It was so loud/noisy. I couldn't hear anything.
25. We haven't heard from him for a long time.
26. I don't have to hear it.
27. His hearing isn't good. He needs hearing aids.
28. I haven't heard that since high school.
    -Neither have I.
29. Nobody can hear us.
30. I didn't hear it. What did you say?
31. Do I have to hear it?
32. Can you hear me?
33. Do you hear that?
34. What did you hear? Where did you hear that?
35. I have good news and bad news. Which one do you want to (/would you like to) hear first?
36. Did you hear that? We (have) won!
37. He's going to retire. Are you hearing this?
38. Can I hear it?
39. Can you tell me what you heard?
40. Didn't you hear me?
41. When can I hear from you?
42. Just hear me out, will you?
43. Can you hear me out?
44. I think we should hear him out.
45. Why don't you hear him out?

## Unit 6

1. I want you to go. I can't talk to you now.
2. I want Jenny to come to the party. Can you invite her?
3. I want you to stay away from him. Do you hear me?

4. You want us to get along, don't you?
5. I want you to think about it.
6. I want you to say whatever is on your mind. You can be honest with me.
7. I want you to tell him.
8. I want you to calm down.
9. I want him to love me back. Is it so wrong?
10. I want him to pay. I want him to suffer.
11. I want everyone to know the truth.
12. I want you to know how sorry I am for everything.
13. I wanted you to know how sorry I was.
14. I wanted him to know how much I loved him.
15. I want you to know I'm here for you.
16. He wants us to finish this by today. We have no time to waste.
    (We don't have (any) time to waste.)
17. I want you to do the right thing.
18. I want you to support me. I want you to be on my side. That's all I want.
19. I want you to wait for me.
20. This is for you. He would want you to have it.
21. He expects me to do everything for him.
22. I expect you to do better.
23. I need you to trust/believe me. Can you do that for me?
24. I need you to come (and) get me. I want to (/would like to) get out of here.
25. I want this to work (so) badly. I want it to go well.
26. I wanted you to be the first to know.
27. I want there to be hope.
28. I'm not religious (or anything). But I want there to be an afterlife.
29. I want you to be on your best behavior today. Can I count on you?
30. I want you to be nice to your sister/brother.
31. I want you to be happy.
32. I want him to be safe.
33. I just want you to be honest with me.
34. I want you to be brave. Can you do that for me?
35. I want it to be a dream. I want everything to go back to the way it was.
36. I want everything to be perfect.
37. I want my life to be better. I want my life to mean something.
38. Everybody wants the world to be better. We are making the world a better place every/each day.
39. He wants you to be his girlfriend.
40. I wanted it to be him. I wanted him to be the one.
41. I don't want you to go. I want you to stay with me.

## 정답 체크

42. I don't want you to get hurt.
43. I don't want you to get the wrong idea.
44. I don't want you to do anything you are not comfortable with.
45. Can you not tell anyone? I don't want anyone to know I'm here.
46. I don't want him to get the wrong idea. I don't want him to misunderstand.
47. I don't want us to fight anymore.
48. I don't want anyone to see me like this.
49. I don't want you to waste any more time.
50. I don't want you to feel pressured.
51. I don't want you to be angry.
52. I don't want you to be hard on yourself. Nobody saw it coming. (No one could see it coming.)
53. I don't want you to be self-conscious.
54. I don't want us to be friends. I want us to grow old together.
55. I don't need you to save me. I can save myself.
56. I don't want it to be true.
57. I don't want you to be perfect. Nobody is perfect. I just want you to be yourself.
58. I didn't want to tell you. I didn't want you to feel bad.
59. I didn't want anyone to know.
60. I didn't tell you. (Because) I didn't want you to worry.
61. I don't expect you to do anything. Do whatever you want to do.
62. I don't expect you to understand.
63. I can't expect him to do this for me. He's not reliable.
64. We shouldn't expect him to do all the work. He's not a machine.
65. Don't expect other people to be like you.
66. We shouldn't expect people to change for us.
67. I didn't expect him to come.
68. I didn't expect anyone to help me. I don't need anyone to save me.
69. Nobody expects you to do anything you are not comfortable with.
70. You can't expect everyone to like you. It's not possible.
71. Do you want me to come with you?
72. Do you want me to get you anything?
73. Do you want me to stay?
74. Do you want me to drive?
75. Do you want me to pull over?
76. Do you want me to help you?
77. Do you want me to take a picture of you?
78. Do you want me to call a cab?
79. Do you want me to do something? Do you want me to beat him up?
80. Is there anything you want me to do? What do you want me to do?

81. Do you want me to cover for you?
82. Do you want me to talk/speak to him?
83. Do you want it to happen again?
84. Do you want everyone to know? Just act normal.
85. What do you want me to say? What do you expect me to say?
    Tell me and I will say it.
86. Do you want me to text you the address?
87. What did you want me to do?
88. Did you want me to lie?
89. What do you expect me to do?
90. Okay, what do you need me to do?
91. Would you like me to make you some tea?
92. Would you like me to arrange a meeting?
93. Would you like me to bring anything/something?
94. Would you like me to do it for you?
95. How would you like me to handle this?
96. Would you like me to stop?
97. Would you like me to say something?
98. Would you like me to send you the link?
99. Would you like me to show you how to use that?
100. You're amazing, talented, and (you) have so much potential.
    Would you like me to go on?

**Review**

1. I think we should help him.
2. If you ask him, he will help you.
3. I can help you with the project.
   -Can you? Thank you.
4. You have to help me.
5. I have been helping my mom with groceries.
6. Sorry. I was just trying to help.
7. You (have) helped me immensely. Thank you so much.
8. I didn't do it alone. My friend helped me.
9. I was going to help you with that.
10. I know. It helps with digestion. It helps a lot.
    -Does it?
11. Take this with water. It's going to (/will) help you with your headache.
12. It might/may help you sleep. Why don't you try it?
13. Regular exercise will (/is going to) help you overcome depression.

## 정답 체크

14. You want me to help you, don't you?
15. I just wanted to help.
16. Everybody needs help sometimes. Why don't you let me help you?
17. You don't have to help me. I can manage.
18. Sorry, I couldn't help you.
19. It isn't going to (/won't) help me sleep.
20. I'm not helping, am I? Sorry, I'll get out of your way.
21. I don't want anyone to help me. I can do it myself.
22. He didn't use to help (me) around the house, either.
23. It doesn't help.
    -Doesn't it?
24. It didn't help at all. It made it even worse.
25. I'm afraid I can't help you.
26. He took out the trash for the first time. He hadn't helped (me) before.
27. I don't know how we can help him.
28. Can (/Could) you help me with this?
29. Do you want me to (/Shall I) help you with that?
30. Does your husband help (you) around the house?
31. Did it help?
32. Were you going to help me? When were you going to do that?
33. Does it help?
34. Do you think it'll help?
35. How do you think we should help?
36. Are you going to help me or not?
37. Why didn't anyone help him?
38. What will help with constipation?
39. Who helped you? Do you know who did?
40. I know I shouldn't laugh. But I can't help it.
41. I shouldn't eat anymore. I can't help it.
42. I can't help feeling sad.
43. Excuse me, I couldn't help overhearing your conversation.
44. I couldn't help noticing you. You're so beautiful.
45. I couldn't help feeling sorry for myself.

## Unit 7

1. I told him to hurry (up). He'll (/is going to) be down in a minute.
2. Tim told me to read it. I read it and loved it (/and liked it so much).
3. I told Tim to (come and) pick us up. He'll (/is going to) be here soon.
4. Tim just called. I told him to call us back.

5. I told you to bring it, didn't I?
6. He told us to follow him.
7. I told you to put these away. Why haven't you done it yet?
8. I told you to try it.
9. I told Sarah to get ready an hour ago. Why is she taking so long to get ready?
10. We told him to take it. So, he has it.
11. You told me to do this. That's why I did it.
12. He told me to wait here. That's why I'm waiting here.
13. I told him to have it. That's why he has it.
14. You told me to go there. That's why I went there.
15. You told me to tell him. That's why I told him.
16. Jim asked me to come. That's why I'm here. (That's why I came.)
17. Kim asked me to do this (for her). That's why I'm doing this.
18. You told me to buy it. That's why I got/bought this.
19. He told us to change the title. That's why we're changing it again.
20. He (has) always encouraged me to believe in myself and achieve my goals. That's why I respect him.
21. I asked him to help. We need all the help we can get.
22. Sean asked me to look out for you.
23. I asked him to stay. I didn't want to be alone.
24. He asked/told me to stay with you. He really cares about you.
25. You asked/told me to give it to you. I know this is your favorite.
26. He asked her to marry him. They're going to get married next month. (They're getting married next month.)
27. I told him to be quiet.
28. He told me to be myself.
29. I told them to be careful. I was so worried about them.
30. I asked/told you to be nice to him. I (only) asked you to do one thing, and you couldn't even do that (for me).
31. He told me to ask you. Can you help?
32. He told me to let go. I know I should, but it's so hard.
33. They were getting anxious. I told them to be patient.
34. He was (being) nosy. I told him to mind his own business.
35. You told me to try something new. It was good advice.
36. He told me to tell you. I think he really likes you.
37. I asked/told him to give us more time.
38. He told me to choose/pick one. I don't know which one I want to (/would like to) pick/choose.
39. You told me to buy/get anything I want. Did I spend too much?
40. They all told me to ignore that. But it's not easy when it's right in your face.

## 정답 체크

41. He seemed unsure about it, so I told him to think about it.
42. He told me to trust my instinct. I'm going with my gut on this.
    (I'm going to go with my gut on this.)
43. He taught me to do this.
44. He begged her to take him back. I don't know what happened after.
45. He asked me to look into it.
46. He advised me to wait until I'm ready.
47. He persuaded me to accept the job offer. He talked me into it.
48. The doctor advised him to lose weight.
49. The doctor told you to exercise. You need to listen to him.
50. The doctor told him to quit smoking. And he gave up smoking last April.
51. I told you not to do that, didn't I?
52. He asked me not to go.
53. Keep still. He told us not to move.
54. I told you not to speak/talk to strangers.
55. I told you not to laugh. Stop it! I'm serious.
56. He told us not to wait (for him). He's going to (/will) be late.
57. I told you not to worry about it. There's no need to worry.
58. He told us not to hurry. He told us to take our time.
59. The doctor told us not to open the window. We have to keep warm.
60. He told me not to eat meat.
61. He told me not to lose hope. But I feel hopeless.
62. You told me not to come today. Don't you remember?
63. I asked you not to tell anyone. I don't understand why you told him.
64. You asked me not to say anything. I'm not going to say anything.
65. Jim told us not to use this. We shouldn't use it.
66. I warned you not to trust/believe him. He's a cheater.
67. I told you not to hang out with them.
68. I told him not to contact me again.
69. I told him not to lie. I hate lies.
70. He begged me not to go. It was so hard to leave him.
71. You told me not to bother you. That's why I didn't tell you earlier.
72. I told him not to brag. He's such a show-off.
73. He told me not to be afraid of change.
74. He told me not to be scared of it. He told me to face my fears.
75. He told us not to be late. We should leave soon.
76. I warned you not to do that.
77. You told me not to change anything.
78. I told him not to ruin this.
79. He told me not to forget.

80. I told you not to interrupt (me) while I'm working. What's so urgent?
81. I didn't tell you to wait for me. You didn't have to wait.
82. I didn't tell him to do that. What are you talking about/saying?
83. I didn't ask him to help. (I haven't asked him to help.)
84. He didn't tell us to bring it. Did we have to bring it?
85. I didn't ask you to do anything.
86. I didn't tell you to do this. Sorry, I forgot to mention it.
87. He didn't tell me to call. I'm not going to call him until he calls me first.
88. He didn't force me to come. I wanted to be/come here.
89. Nobody forced me to do this. It was my decision. I (will) take full responsibility.
90. Nobody taught me to do this. It was self-taught.
91. Did you tell him to go? Why did you do that?
92. Then, why did you tell me to do that?
93. When did I tell you to do that?
94. What did he advise you to do?
95. Tell me. What did I ask/tell you to do?
96. Did I tell you to come today?
97. Did you just ask me to help you?
98. How many times have I told you not to do that?
99. Who told you to do that?
100. Didn't you tell me to come by 2?

**Review**

1. You can try it.
2. I might/may try a new hobby.
3. I'll try it again later.
4. I like trying new things. (I like to try new things.)
5. I know you have been trying hard. (I know you tried hard.)
6. I (have) tried everything.
7. I tried it, but it didn't work.
8. I was trying something different.
9. You should try it.
10. I have to try harder, don't I? (I should try harder, shouldn't I?)
11. I would try my best.
12. We might as well try it while we are here.
13. He's trying to make it work. And so am I.
14. I want to (/would like to) try something new.
15. You told me to try it.
    -Did I?

## 정답 체크

16. I want you to try it.
17. I'm trying.
18. I don't want to (/wouldn't like to) try anymore.
19. It was my first time. I hadn't tried it before.
20. You aren't trying hard enough.
21. We haven't tried that yet.
22. I wasn't trying to do anything.
23. He doesn't try anymore.
24. I'm not trying to stop you.
25. Don't try this at home.
26. You shouldn't try anything stupid.
27. Do you want to (/Would you like to) try it?
28. Can (/Could/May) I try it?
29. Do you think I should try it?
30. Do you want me to try it?
31. What are you trying to do?
32. What were you trying to do?
33. Have you tried it (before)?
34. Did you try it? (Have you tried it?)
35. Why don't you try it?
36. Are you going to try it?
37. Do you think you'll try it?
38. What are you trying to say?
39. Didn't you tell me to try it?
40. Why did he try to kill himself?
41. Why try? Why bother?
42. You wouldn't understand.
    -Try me!
43. Nobody will (/is going to/would) believe me.
    -Try me. I might.
44. You should try it. It's worth a try.
45. Well, it was worth a try. I had to try it.

## Unit 8

1. He said it was good. I agree with him.
2. He said he was 36 (years old). And I told him he didn't look his age.
3. A friend of mine said this book was great/good. He recommended it to me.
4. I told you it was too small. We need something bigger.

5. He said it was urgent. You should call him now.
6. I said I was sorry. What more do you want from me?
7. You said you were hungry. Why aren't you eating?
8. He said it was difficult/hard.
9. He said you were very helpful. Thank you for helping him.
10. They said it was next Saturday, didn't they?
11. He said it was free.
12. He said he was disappointed. I feel so bad. I let him down.
13. Everyone said it was impossible to do (that). But I did not care.
14. You said it was a mistake. It was a mistake, wasn't it?
15. I told you it was too late.
16. He said he was unhappy there. He told me he wanted to quit (his job).
17. I told him there was nothing (/wasn't anything) to worry.
18. Carol said there wasn't a problem. And I believe her.
19. I already asked him. He said he wasn't quite ready.
20. He said there were many people. I don't know if/whether I want to (/would like to) go.
21. He said I looked young.
22. You said you needed this, so I got/bought it for you.
23. He said he loved/liked it. I was happy to see his smile.
    (I was happy to see him smile.)
24. Jim told me he knew. I didn't know he knew.
25. You said you had it. What happened to it? Did you lose it?
26. You said you didn't like it. What changed your mind?
27. I said I didn't regret anything.
28. You said you didn't know anything about that. That's why I didn't ask you.
29. Ted said he didn't have time. He told me he couldn't help.
    (He said he couldn't help.)
30. He said he didn't remember. I didn't want to ask anymore.
31. He said we had to be/come here by 2. Where's everyone?
32. My friend said you could fix this.
33. You said you wanted to go there with me.
34. You said you would (/were going to) call last night. I waited for your call.
35. He said he was working. He told me he was busy.
36. He said he wanted to meet you.
37. I told you I could help. (I said I could help you.) Why don't you let me help (you)?
38. I said I would (/was going to) do it later. Just leave it.
39. I told him I had to go somewhere, and I left.
40. He said he would (/was going to) pick it up.
41. He told me to ask you. He said you would know.
42. Bill said you were waiting for me here. What's up?

## 정답 체크

43. He said I could get a refund.
44. I told you everything would (/was going to) work out.
45. You said you wanted to do this, didn't you?
46. He said it would take about 3 hours. And he said it wouldn't cost much.
47. You said you had to work. Aren't you supposed to be at work now?
48. He said everything was going well.
49. You said you understood me. Was that a lie, too?
50. Someone said I could use this coupon here. Can I use it?
51. He said he would let us know soon.
52. You said you could go with me.
53. Jenny told me she was studying with her friends. She said she would be late.
54. He said we could do it online. Why hadn't I thought about it before?
55. You said I would get it today.
56. Gary told me there would be enough time.
57. I told him to leave me alone. I said I wanted to be alone.
58. He told me he had to run some errands.
59. I told him not to do that. I said he was wasting his time.
60. I said I loved him. Was it too soon?
61. Tom said he couldn't come.
62. You said I didn't have to do that.
63. He assured me there wouldn't be a problem. It's odd.
64. I told you I didn't want to do it.
65. I said you didn't have to worry about it anymore. Trust me.
66. He said he wasn't doing anything. He said he was free.
67. You said you wouldn't do that again. You promised.
68. He said I couldn't cancel it.
69. He said he wasn't going to come.
    (He said he wasn't coming. / He said he wouldn't come.)
70. He said he didn't want to see me anymore.
71. He said he had lost his keys.
72. I told him I had forgotten. I told him the truth.
73. He said he had finished work, and he was on his/the way.
74. He told me he had known it for a while.
75. He said he had already seen the movie.
76. I told you I hadn't done it.
77. Mark said he hadn't said anythig to him  (he hadn't told him anything).
    I don't think he told him.
78. He said he hadn't seen you that day.
79. He told me it hadn't been easy. He said he had been going through a hard time.
80. You said you hadn't done this before.

81. I didn't say I wanted to do this.
82. I didn't say it was urgent.
83. I didn't say it was the only way. There are other ways to do this.
84. I didn't say it was bad. It is neither good nor bad.
85. He didn't say it was going to (/would) be hard.
86. You didn't say you had done/tried it.
87. He didn't say it was your fault. I think you misunderstood.
88. I didn't say it was impossible.
89. I didn't say I would (/was going to) do it. I said I was thinking about it.
90. No one said I could do this. But I knew I could (do it). I believed in myself.
91. Did you say it was today? What time did you say it was?
92. Did he say you would need this?
93. What time did you say I had to be/go there?
94. When did you say you would call (me)?
95. When did you say you were meeting him?
    (When did you say you would[/were going to] meet him?)
96. Which one did you say you wanted to have?
97. Did I say I was sorry?
98. Where did you say you were going?
99. Didn't you say you could come?
100. Didn't you say you wanted it?

**Review**

1. Be careful! It might/may break.
2. It's so fragile. It breaks easily.
3. We broke up.
4. It can break down again.
5. Nothing will (/is going to/can) break him. He's so strong.
6. Stop saying that. You're breaking my heart.
7. It broke my heart.
   –Did it?
8. Don't tell him. It would (/will/is going to) break his heart.
9. He said it had broken down.
10. I told you not to break it.
11. It used to break down all the time.
12. It's breaking my heart to see you like this. (It breaks my heart to see you like this.)
13. I don't want you to break it.
14. I didn't break it. It wasn't me.
15. It won't break. It's impossible to break.

## 정답 체크

16. He doesn't break promises. He never does.
17. You have never broken promises.
18. I couldn't break my promise.
19. I don't want to (/wouldn't like to) break my promise to him.
20. I'm not breaking the law.
21. We can't break the law. And neither can you.
22. I wasn't breaking the law.
23. I don't know how it broke.
24. I'm not going to break his heart. I can't do it.
25. Don't break my heart.
26. Are you breaking up with me?
27. Why did you break up with him?
28. Didn't you break up with him?
29. Do you want to break up with him?
30. Who broke it? Did you break it?
31. Did it break down again?
32. Were you going to break it?
33. Do you think it'll break?
34. Do you want me to break it? (Shall I break it?)
35. Do you know who broke it?
36. Why do you break your promises?
37. How many glasses have you broken?
38. We need a breakthrough.
39. This is a breakthrough!
40. Everybody, it's a breakthrough moment. Let's celebrate.
41. It was a huge breakthrough in science.
42. It might/may be a/the breakthrough I've been waiting for.

## Unit 9

1. I asked him how much it was. He said it was 45,000 won.
2. He asked me where it was. I said I didn't know.
3. I asked you how it was. And you said it was fun.
4. He asked me where you were, and I told him you were at work.
5. I asked him how old he was. He said he was 29 (years old).
6. I asked him when it was, and he said it was next Monday.
7. He asked me what it was, and I couldn't answer.
8. I asked him how much it would be, and he said it wouldn't be expensive.
9. He asked me what your name was.
10. I asked him what he was worried about.

11. He asked me how long it had been like this. I didn't know what to say.
12. He asked me what my plan was. I couldn't say anything because I didn't have one (/a plan/any plans).
13. He asked me what my religion was.
14. I asked him how he had been. He said he had been well.
15. I asked him when it would be ready. He told me it would be ready in an hour.
16. He asked me where I was from. I told him I was (a) Korean.
17. I asked him when he would (/was going to) be/come back. He said he didn't know.
18. I asked myself why I was so angry. There was no (/wasn't a) reason to be angry.
19. I wanted to ask you when this would be over.
20. I asked him what his favorite color was. He said it was yellow.
21. I asked him what I needed.
22. I asked him what he was doing. He said he was working.
23. I asked him how long it would take to get/go there. He said it would take 2 hours.
24. He asked me how much it cost to change (that).
    (He asked me how much it would cost if he changed it.)
25. He asked me where I had been
26. I asked him how he had become so successful.
27. I asked him what he wanted to say.
    He said there wasn't anything (/was nothing) he wanted to say.
28. He asked (me) what I liked, and what I did on weekends.
    He asked me lots of/many/a lot of questions.
29. He asked me when I had come. He also asked me how I had come/got(ten) here.
30. I asked him where he had bought/got it. He said he couldn't remember.
31. I asked you what you were going to do tomorrow.
32. He asked me how long I had been waiting.
33. He asked me where I would (/was going to) be, so I told him I would (/was going to) be here.
34. I asked you why you had to do that. You didn't quite answer my question.
35. He asked me what I was going to wear.
36. What if he asks me what happened? What do I say? (What can/should/shall I say?)
37. What if he asks me why I blocked him? What am I going to say?
    (What shall I say?/What do you want me to say?)
38. What if he asks you where you were? Are you going to lie?
39. What if he asks you why you haven't done it yet?
40. What if he asks me why you didn't come?
41. I asked him when he would (/was going to) do it.
    He said he would (/was going to) do it this weekend.
42. I asked him which one I had to buy.
43. He asked me where I was going. But I didn't want to answer.

## 정답 체크

44. He asked me when you could come.
45. He asked me where you lived. I didn't tell him.
46. He asked me what I had seen. I said I hadn't seen anything.
47. He asked me how long we had known each other.
48. I wanted to ask you what you would do if the roles were reversed.
49. I wanted to ask you what you wanted (to have) for your birthday.
50. I wanted to ask him why he couldn't do it, but I couldn't (ask).
51. He asked me what time we would come tomorrow, and I said we would be/go there at two.
52. He asked me what you liked. I think he likes you.
53. I asked him how he made it.
54. I asked you what you were doing.
55. I asked him where he worked, but he didn't answer.
56. I asked him what I could do for him, but he said there was nothing (/wasn't anything) I could do.
57. He asked me what I had done with it. I didn't know what to say.
58. I asked him how much I had to pay, and he said we didn't have to pay.
59. I asked him where he was going to go, who he was going to go with, and when he was going to come back.
60. He asked me where I wanted to go, what I wanted to do, where I wanted to stay, and how long I could stay.
61. I asked him if/whether it was too big, and he said it was okay.
62. I asked him if/whether someone was using this. He said nobody was (using it).
63. I asked him if/whether he could fix it. He said he couldn't.
64. I asked him if/whether he had done it before. And he said he hadn't tried/done it.
65. I asked him if/whether he liked it. He said he did. (He said he liked it.)
66. I asked you if/whether you wanted to do it. You said you did.
67. I asked him if/whether there was enough time, and he said there was.
68. He asked me if/whether I could think about it, and I said I would (think about it).
69. I asked him if/whether I could do that, and he said I could.
70. I asked him if/whether he meant it. He said he meant it. (He said he did.)
71. I asked you if/whether you had been there. Didn't you say you hadn't been there?
72. He asked me if/whether you could come.
73. He asked me if/whether I was coming (/would come/was going to come) tomorrow. I told him I was thinking about it.
74. He asked me if/whether I could understand him. I don't know if/whether I can understand him.
75. I asked him if/whether he loved me.
76. He asked me if/whether I was Japanese.
77. He asked me if/whether I had used it.

78. He asked me if/whether we had been waiting long.
79. I asked you if/whether you wanted it. You said you didn't need it.
80. I asked him if/whether he knew you. He told me he did. (He said he knew you.)
81. You didn't ask me what I needed. You never do.
82. He didn't ask me if/whether I could come. He didn't invite me.
83. I didn't ask what his thoughts were (/what his thought was).
    I asked you what you thought. Tell me what you want to (/would like to) do.
84. You didn't even ask me how I was feeling (/I felt).
    Don't you want to know how I'm feeling (/I feel)?
85. I couldn't ask him if/whether he could forgive me.
86. I didn't ask him why he wanted to do that.
    Why hadn't I thought to ask that simple question?
87. Don't ask me if/whether I'm okay. I don't know how to answer that right now.
88. He didn't ask me how my day was. And neither did I. We stopped communicating.
89. I can't ask (him) how much money he makes, can I?
90. We shouldn't ask people how old they are or what they do (for a living).
    It can be impolite when you meet them for the first time.
91. Did you ask him what he wanted to have?
92. Did you ask him when he was going to come?
93. Did you ask him where he was?
94. Did you ask him why he was doing that?
95. Did you ask him what we had to do?
96. Did you ask him if/whether we could stay here?
97. Did you ask him if/whether it was okay?
98. Did you ask him when it would be?
99. Did I ask you how you were (doing)?
100. Didn't we ask him if/whether he could help us?

**Review**

1. I want to (/would like to) meet him.
2. You might/may meet someone there.
3. You should meet him. You are going to (/will) like him.
4. I can meet you tomorrow.
5. Okay, I'll meet you there.
6. I have met him before.
7. We've been meeting here for a long time.
8. I want you to meet him.
9. I was going to meet my friends after school.
   –Were you?
10. We used to meet every day.

## 정답 체크

11. I like meeting new people. (I like to meet new people.)
12. It was so nice to meet you.
13. You are going to (/will) meet my family soon.
14. We first met in 2010.
15. We meet every Thursday.
16. I look forward to meeting you. (I'm looking forward to meeting you.)
17. It's hard to meet like-minded people.
18. You said you could meet me today.
19. I don't think we should meet anymore.
20. I'm not going to meet him again.
21. I don't want to (/wouldn't like to) meet him again.
22. I can't meet you this week.
23. We haven't met (before).
24. He doesn't meet new people. He's an introvert.
25. You haven't met the right person yet.
26. I didn't meet him. He said he had to work late.
27. I don't think I'll ever meet anyone.
28. I might/may not meet him again.
29. We couldn't meet there.
30. You said you would (/were going to) meet your friends. Where are you going to meet them?
31. Do I have to meet him?
32. When do you think I'll meet the right person?
33. Have you met him?
34. What time do you want to (/would you like to) meet?
35. Where did you meet? How did you meet?
36. Can you meet me later?
37. Where should we meet?
38. Haven't we met before?
39. Don't you want to (/Wouldn't you like to) meet your friends?
40. Come on! Meet me halfway. (Let's meet halfway.)
41. Can you meet me halfway?
42. I'll meet you halfway. How about 150?
43. Why don't we meet halfway?
44. If you can't meet me halfway, it's not going to work.

## Unit 10

1. Sorry, I thought it was mine.
2. I thought you were someone else.

3. I thought it was today. Didn't you say it was today?
4. I thought it was easier. I didn't think it was hard.
5. Everybody thought it would be easy.
6. I thought it was here. It's odd. I thought I had put it here.
7. I thought you were okay. Why didn't you tell me?
8. I thought he was sick. He didn't sound well.
9. I thought it would be impossible to do (that).
10. I really thought it was expensive.
11. I thought you were working. I didn't want to bother you.
12. I thought you had it.
13. We all thought you knew.
14. I thought I knew him. You think you know someone.
15. I thought I could do it for you.
16. He thought I wanted to have it.
17. I thought it would take much longer.
18. I thought it cost a lot to do that.
19. I thought you would call (me).
20. I thought you were going to (/would) come. I was waiting for you.
21. I thought someone else was here.
22. I thought he had to work this weekend.
23. I thought he was going to (/would) help us.
24. I thought you would stop coming.
25. I thought you had thought about it.
26. I thought you had seen me there. Didn't you see me?
27. I thought I had to come today.
28. I thought you wanted to go there.
29. Everyone thought I was going to (/would) lose.
30. I thought we were meeting today.
31. I thought I wanted to do this, but I don't.
32. I thought you had been here before.
33. I thought there would be many people.
34. I thought you said it was okay.
35. I thought you told me to do this first.
36. I thought you understood. I thought you were on my side.
37. We all thought it would work.
38. I thought you were sleeping. I didn't want to wake you up.
39. I thought it was raining.
40. I thought it was over.
41. I thought you would (/were going to) bring it.
42. I thought he was going to (/would) get angry.

## 정답 체크

43. I thought he would (/was going to) change. I believed he could change.
44. I thought it would (/was going to) be different this time.
45. I thought we could spend more time together.
46. I really thought I was going to (/would) get the job.
47. I thought I had done it.
48. You thought I had made it, didn't you?
49. I thought I had made a mistake.
50. I thought you wouldn't want to talk about it.
51. I thought you didn't know.
52. I thought you didn't have it. So, I brought extra.
53. I thought you couldn't eat meat.
54. I thought you didn't want to come. That's why I didn't ask you.
55. I thought you didn't care.
56. I thought you didn't want to see him.
57. I thought you wouldn't like it. I didn't know you liked these kinds of things.
58. I thought I couldn't change it.
59. I thought it didn't matter. I didn't know it was important. (I didn't know it mattered.)
60. I thought he wouldn't mind.
61. I knew you were here.
62. I knew he was going to (/would) come.
63. I knew you would (/were going to) like it.
64. I knew you could do it.
65. I knew he was telling me the truth.
66. I knew he was like that before we got married.
67. I knew I wanted it. I just had to have it.
68. We knew you would (/were going to) win. Congratulations!
69. I knew he couldn't stay. He had told me.
70. You knew I would (/was going to) do this, didn't you?
71. I didn't know you were here. When did you come?
72. I didn't know it was this small.
73. I didn't know I could do this.
74. I didn't know it would turn out like this.
75. I didn't know he would mind.
76. I didn't know you knew about that.
77. I didn't know you liked it.
78. I didn't even know I was doing that.
79. I didn't know I had to go there. I thought you (had) told us not to come.
80. I didn't know you wanted to go there.
81. I didn't know you were coming. Why didn't you say anything?
82. I didn't know he would do that. I didn't think he had the courage.

83. We didn't know we had to pay for that. We thought it was free.
84. I thought you could come. I didn't know you had other plans.
85. I didn't know you were waiting for me.
86. I didn't know there was a problem.
87. I didn't know this could (/would) go viral. We were really lucky.
88. I didn't know you had been there.
89. You didn't know it would happen. It isn't your fault.
90. No one knew it would (/was going to) last that long.
91. How did you know I was here? Who told you that?
92. How did you know I wanted to have this?
93. Did you know you had to work this weekend?
94. Did you know I would (/was going to) call?
95. Did you know she was pregnant?
96. Did you know you could lose everything?
97. Did you know he would succeed? Well, I knew.
98. Did you know it would happen?
99. Didn't you know it was illegal?
100. Did you really think you could (/would) get away with it?

**Review**

1. You can say anything.
   -Can I?
2. I wanted to say thank you.
   -So did I.
3. You have to say something.
4. You can say that again!
5. Say no more! I get it. (I understand.)
6. I was just going to say that.
7. There's something I want to (/would like to) say.
8. You told me not to say anything.
9. I thought you said you didn't like it.
10. As I was saying, it's not a/the problem.
11. I (have) said it all.
12. If you say so. Whatever you say.
13. I didn't say anything.
14. I don't want you to say anything.
15. I wasn't going to say anything.
    -Neither was I.
16. Don't say anything.

## 정답 체크

17. I wasn't saying that.
18. There is nothing (/isn't anything) left to say.
19. I'm not saying it's right.
20. You don't have to say anything. I know.
21. You shouldn't say that.
22. I couldn't say anything.
23. You haven't said a word since you got/came here.
    -Haven't I?
24. I wouldn't say that.
25. Do it now! I will not (/won't/am not going to) say it again.
26. I don't know what he said.
27. Sorry. I didn't mean to say that.
28. What did you say?
29. When did I say that?
30. Can (/Could) you say that again?
31. Can (/Could/May) I say something?
32. What are you going to say?
33. What were you going to say?
34. Is there anything you want to (/would like to) say?
35. What do you want me to say?
36. That's nonsense! Who said that?
37. Who's saying that?
38. What (else/more) is there to say? I have nothing (/don't have anything) to say.
39. What should I say?
40. What are you saying?
41. Why didn't you say it sooner?
42. What can I say?
43. Is that all you have to (/want to) say?
44. Who's to say what's right and what's wrong?
45. Who's to say what's good or bad?

Take the first step. You can do it!

# 나만의 40문장 노트 ✦✦

외우고 싶은 문장이나 잘 기억나지 않는 문장을 적어 두고, 복습이 필요할 때 확인해 보세요.

- [ ]
- [ ]
- [ ]
- [ ]
- [ ]
- [ ]
- [ ]
- [ ]
- [ ]
- [ ]
- [ ]
- [ ]
- [ ]
- [ ]
- [ ]
- [ ]
- [ ]
- [ ]
- [ ]
- [ ]

## 기초영어 1000문장 말하기 연습 4

**초판 제1쇄** 2025년 8월 28일

| | |
|---|---|
| **지은이** | 박미진 |
| **펴낸이** | 서장혁 |
| **편집** | 토마토출판사 편집부 |
| **디자인** | 이새봄 |
| **주소** | 서울 마포구 양화로 161 727호 |
| **TEL** | 1544-5383 |
| **홈페이지** | www.tomato4u.com |
| **E-mail** | support@tomato4u.com |
| **등록** | 2012.1.11. |
| **ISBN** | 979-11-92603-84-1  14740 |

\* 잘못된 책은 구입처에서 교환해드립니다.
\* 가격은 뒤표지에 있습니다.
\* 이 책은 국제저작권법에 의해 보호받으므로 어떠한 형태로든 전재, 복제, 표절을 금합니다.